WHIT
PL

Ted Whitehead

PLAYS

THE FOURSOME
ALPHA BETA
THE SEA ANCHOR
THE PUNISHMENT

OBERON BOOKS
LONDON

First published in this collection in 2005 by Oberon Books Ltd
(incorporating Absolute Classics)
521 Caledonian Road, London N7 9RH
Tel: 020 7607 3637 / Fax: 020 7607 3629
e-mail: oberon.books@btinternet.com
www.oberonbooks.com

The Foursome first published in 1972 by Faber. *Alpha Beta* first
published in 1972 by Faber. *The Sea Anchor* first published in 1975
by Faber. *The Punishment* first published in 1972 by Hutchison's.

A catalogue record for this book is available from the British Library.

Cover illustration: Andrzej Klimowski

Cover typography: Jeff Willis

ISBN: 1 84002 222 1

Printed in Great Britain by Antony Rowe Ltd, Chippenham.

Contents

for Gwenda

THE FOURSOME

Characters

HARRY
early twenties

TIM
late twenties

MARIE
about twenty

BELLA
nineteen

The action takes place in a hollow in the sandhills
at Freshfield, near Liverpool.

The Foursome was first performed at the The Theatre Upstairs at the Royal Court Theatre on 17 March 1971, with the following cast:

HARRY, Paul Angelis

TIM, Philip Donaghy

MARIE, Clare Sutcliffe

BELLA, Sharon Duce

Director Jonathan Hales

Designer John Napier

Lights Liz Wells

This production was presented by Michael Codron, by arrangement with the Royal Court Theatre, at the Fortune Theatre on 4 May 1971. The part of Tim was played by James Hazeldine.

ACT ONE

Before the lights come up, the sound of birds is heard. Then the sound of pop music, slowly getting louder as the lights come up slowly. The lights reach glaring intensity on a scene of baked white sand and blue sky as the music becomes deafening.

HARRY appears at the top of the dune and stands surveying the hollow. He carries a beach bag and a transistor radio. TIM joins him. He carries a beach bag and a wad of newspapers. Both men wear sweatshirts and jeans.

HARRY looks behind across the sand. TIM does the same. They grin at each other. HARRY snaps off the transistor. For a second they stand poised looking at the hollow in silence.

HARRY: OK?
TIM: (*Hesitant. Looking all round the scene.*) Hunh.
HARRY: What?
TIM: You wanna go on a bit?
HARRY: I'm fucked.
TIM: We go further than this.
HARRY: No need.
TIM: We better hang on for them.
HARRY: What are they doing?
TIM: (*Looking.*) They're coming up.
HARRY: I can't see them.
TIM: (*Points.*) They're coming round there.
    (*HARRY jumps down into the hollow. Sprawls on his back. Stares at the sky, stretches his arms.*)
HARRY: (*Luxuriating.*) Ahhhhhhhhhhhhh.
TIM: They're sitting down there.
HARRY: Give them a shout.
    (*TIM waves.*)
    (*Shouts.*) Now arse!
TIM: They'll hear you.
HARRY: (*Shouts.*) NOW ARSE!
TIM: They heard you.
HARRY: They'd hear me whisper. (*Whispers.*) Now arse...

TIM: They're not moving.

HARRY: They're playing hard to get. (*HARRY empties his bag and begins to spread a towel.*) Come on...give us a hand...

TIM: Now they'll stay down there.

HARRY: You bet?

(*TIM comes down and helps HARRY to lay out the things.*) They're gasping for it.

TIM: Yours is.

HARRY: So is yours.

TIM: (*Grins; prissy.*) So am I...

HARRY: (*Grins; prissy.*) So am I, dear...

TIM: Everybody's gasping for it... (*HARRY stretches.*)

HARRY: (*Ecstatic.*) Goddddddd.

(*Both men sprawl on their towels, left stage.*)

TIM: It's gonna be a scorcher.

HARRY: No...serious like...I think you're on there, mate.

TIM: (*Unsure.*) Hunh.

HARRY: I think you're definitely on...don't you?

TIM: I'll tear the arse off it.

HARRY: (*Laughs; prissy.*) Save some for me, sweetheart...

TIM: (*Prissy.*) For you I'll draw on me reserves...

HARRY: (*Laughing.*) Second shot's best.

TIM: You know what she said last night?

HARRY: (*Giggly.*) Go on...

TIM: She said I looked like a...when we were lying in the back of the van...

HARRY: (*Coy.*) I remember...

TIM: She said I looked like a Spaniard.

HARRY: (*Wide-eyed.*) A bullfighter!

TIM: No, a Spaniard.

HARRY: (*Prissy.*) She meant a bullfighter. That's all these cows think about...bullfighters.

TIM: (*Mock-vain.*) Mind you...I think there is a bit of the Spaniard in me.

HARRY: I think there was a bit of the Spaniard in her too.

TIM: (*Mock-angry.*) Oh yeah...I saw you piping...in the mirror.

HARRY: All I could see was a big white arse.

TIM: (*Prissy.*) Well it wasn't mine.

HARRY: (*Prissy.*) I *knew* it wasn't yours, of course.

TIM: Huh!

HARRY: Anyway...you can talk...I drove fourteen times round the Pier Head while you were at it.

TIM: You got stuck on the roundabout.

HARRY: Who got stuck on the roundabout?

(*Both men laugh. Pause.*)

It's gonna be a great day.

TIM: Did *you* get it away?

HARRY: What?

TIM: Last night...did you get your end away?

HARRY: (*Mock-shock.*) I'd only just met her.

TIM: Did that worry you?

HARRY: No...it worried her.

TIM: (*Ironic.*) She looked a bit shy...

HARRY: I think she had the rags up.

TIM: (*Prissy.*) And how would you know?

HARRY: I had a bit of finger pie.

TIM: (*Laughing.*) Did you lick your fingers after?

(*HARRY laughs and lies loudly sniffing his fingers.*)

(*Laughing.*) The van smelt like a fish shop after.

HARRY: (*Wry.*) It smells like a bloody scent counter this morning.

TIM: (*Wry.*) Yeah...they...

(*Pause.*)

HARRY: Pass us an orange.

(*TIM takes an orange from the bag and throws it to HARRY – wide. HARRY catches it.*)

(*Generous.*) Have one yourself.

TIM: Gee thanks, kid.

(*TIM takes an orange. They eat.*)

HARRY: Where are they?

TIM: Waiting for us.

HARRY: They'll have to wait.

(*Pause. TIM collects the orange peel and puts it in a paper bag.*)

(*Mock-stern.*) And don't forget…we swap over at three o'clock.

TIM: Right, captain.

HARRY: Regardless.

TIM: Definitely. (*Pause.*) Hey…

HARRY: What?

TIM: Not if yours has got the rags up.

HARRY: (*Laughing.*) Oh me darling!

(*HARRY grabs TIM, and both men fall back, wrestling and laughing.*)

(*Mock-Irish.*) Ye're all right dere…I'm telling you, lad… dere's no need to be worrying yerself…ye're all right dere…trust ould Danny…

TIM: Who's ould Danny when he's out?

HARRY: How would I know?

(*Both men lie back. HARRY fiddles with the transistor.*)

Where the fuck are they?

TIM: Go and get them.

HARRY: (*Prissy.*) You go.

TIM: You picked them up…

HARRY: (*Arch.*) They picked me up really.

(*TIM goes to the top of the dune and looks across.*)

(*Shouts.*) NOW ARSE!

TIM: Shut up.

HARRY: What?

TIM: They're coming up.

HARRY: Sit down. (*Pause. TIM waves.*)

TIM: They look shagged.

HARRY: They must be psychic. (*TIM stands waving.*)

Sit down.

TIM: They're waving.

HARRY: Come down.

(*TIM comes down.*)

TIM: I'm dying for a burst…

HARRY: (*Mocking.*) Are you all excited?

TIM: (*Mock giggles.*) Ohhh…I'll wet meself in a minute!

(*TIM goes off left to the woods.*

HARRY lies back and closes his eyes.

After a minute the girls appear, close together. Both are very heavily made up, with hair lacquered and piled high. They wear tight sweaters and mini-skirts and heeled shoes. Each carries a tiny handbag.

They look at HARRY.

HARRY grins extravagantly and waves.

They clamber down daintily.)

MARIE: Jesus...we shoulda brought a rope.

HARRY: Watch you don't twist anything.

(*MARIE staggers the last few steps and falls on HARRY. He grabs her.*)

(*Passionate.*) You're mine, mine, mine!

MARIE: (*Delighted.*) Sod off!

(*The girls sit down, stage right. MARIE rubs her legs. BELLA lies back.*)

Me legs is killing me.

HARRY: Want me to rub them for you?

MARIE: I'm in enough trouble...

HARRY: Relax and strip off.

MARIE: It's far enough, isn't it?

HARRY: (*Coy.*) If we go any farther we'll end up in the woods...

MARIE: I thought that was the idea?

HARRY: What? Yeah...to end up there...not to spend all day there...

MARIE: (*Giggling.*) Hear that, Bella?

BELLA: What?

MARIE: We're gonna end up in the woods.

BELLA: Where's your mate?

HARRY: In the woods.

BELLA: (*Grinning.*) What...already?

HARRY: He couldn't wait.

MARIE: (*Lying back.*) Jesus...I'm beat.

HARRY: Relax...take your clothes off.

MARIE: He wants a free show.

HARRY: (*Coy.*) I'll show you mine...if you'll show me yours.

MARIE: Me mam told me about boys like you.

HARRY: How did she know?

(*HARRY rolls across and tries to kiss MARIE. She struggles, laughing.*)

You're mine.

MARIE: Leggo! You're hurting me hand.

HARRY: Give us a kiss.

MARIE: (*Laughing.*) Sod off!

HARRY: Resistance is useless.

MARIE: Help!

HARRY: Who can help you now?

TIM: (*Entering.*) I!

HARRY: Curses! Returned!

(*TIM leaps down and engages HARRY in a mock sword fight. He pushes HARRY down and transfixes him.*)

TIM: Die, dog!

HARRY: (*Sprawling.*) Ahhhhhhhhh!

(*HARRY dies then pushes TIM over.*)

TIM: You're dead.

HARRY: I recovered.

TIM: (*Mock-huffy.*) If you won't be dead I'm not playing with you...

HARRY: (*Indulgent.*) All right...all right then...

TIM: She's mine.

HARRY: All right...

MARIE: What?

TIM: You're mine.

MARIE: Am I?

(*TIM tries to straddle her. MARIE throws him off.*)

TIM: You're mine now.

MARIE: Sod off!

TIM: (*Protesting.*) I saved you from a fate worse than death.

MARIE: Thanks very much.

TIM: And that's all I get?

HARRY: Wasn't worth saving.

TIM: Wasting me time.

HARRY: Ungrateful bitch.

MARIE: Very nice!

TIM: (*Intense.*) Seriously though...

HARRY: Eh?

TIM: Would you shaft her?

HARRY: (*Pointing to MARIE.*) Her?

TIM: Yeah. Would you shaft her?

HARRY: You mean…

TIM: Would you?

HARRY: (*Reflective.*) You mean if…if I loved her…

TIM: Of course.

HARRY: …and she loved me…

TIM: …and you were married…

HARRY: …and she was a Catholic… (*Pause. HARRY reflects.*)

TIM: (*Eager.*) Would you?

HARRY: (*Snaps.*) Right here on this blanket.

TIM: (*Mock-lecherous.*) Here…in front of us?

HARRY: (*Shy.*) Well…I mean…you wouldn't mind, would you? Would you?

TIM: Not if it was well done.

HARRY: (*Smug.*) You know me…

TIM: I don't know her…

HARRY: That's true. (*Pause. He looks at MARIE.*) Are you good at it?

MARIE: (*Giggles.*) Find out.

HARRY: Right.

(*HARRY throws himself on MARIE. They wrestle. He pins her down.*)

MARIE: He's crazy.

HARRY: D'you fancy a bit?

MARIE: Sod off!

TIM: Don't excite him.

MARIE: He's exciting himself.

TIM: (*Asking a favour.*) No…go easy with him. He's me only mate.

MARIE: Ow! Leggo!

TIM: (*Whispering.*) Go easy…

MARIE: Tell him to let go.

TIM: He takes fits.

MARIE: Does he?

TIM: He foams at the thighs.

MARIE: (*Struggling.*) I think he's taking one now. (*HARRY suddenly releases her and lies back.*)

HARRY: (*Drawls.*) Ahhh...God...that's better. I feel better for that.

MARIE: (*Laughing.*) Are you all right now?

HARRY: That does a chap the world of good. Ahhh.
    (*HARRY stretches and yawns luxuriously.*)

MARIE: Do you come here every weekend?

HARRY: (*Still the drawl.*) Only if we pick anything up on Saturday night.

MARIE: Huh!

HARRY: (*Smug.*) We're very selective...

MARIE: (*Dry.*) Oh I'm made up.

HARRY: We don't just pick anyone up...

MARIE: Thanks.

HARRY: Pleasure.

MARIE: What's my name?

HARRY: Don't you know?

MARIE: I'm asking you.

HARRY: How would I know?

MARIE: I told you last night.

HARRY: There's no need to burst into tears.

MARIE: (*Laughing.*) You don't remember.

HARRY: How could I forget?

MARIE: Do you?

HARRY: Of course I do.

MARIE: What is it then?

HARRY: Of course I remember. (*Pause.*) Albert.

MARIE: Cheeky sod!

HARRY: What's the matter?

MARIE: Last night you kept calling me Nelly.

HARRY: I was pissed.

MARIE: (*Sarcastic.*) Were you...really?
    (*HARRY lies back and closes his eyes.*)

HARRY: This is what I need.
    (*TIM glances at a newspaper. MARIE looks in the beach bag.*)

MARIE: Got any butties?

TIM: What do you want?

MARIE: What are they?

TIM: There's cheese and tomato...or tomato and cheese.

(*MARIE takes a long drink from the bottle of lemonade.*)

Go easy...there's all day.

MARIE: I'm dead thirsty.

TIM: Have an orange.

MARIE: Ta.

(*TIM gives her an orange. She tosses the peel aside.*)

BELLA: Give us a slice.

MARIE: Have an orange.

BELLA: I only want a slice.

(*MARIE gives her a slice.*)

MARIE: I'm burning... Jesus...

HARRY: Take your stockings off.

MARIE: Aye aye.

HARRY: It's gonna get hotter.

MARIE: He's off again.

HARRY: You'll sweat like hell.

MARIE: I'm all right.

TIM: (*To BELLA.*) Why don't you?

BELLA: What?

TIM: Take your stockings off. Get your legs brown.

HARRY: You'll sweat to death if you don't.

BELLA: Are you, Marie?

MARIE: (*To HARRY.*) What about you?

HARRY: What?

MARIE: You'll sweat to death.

HARRY: You want me to strip?

MARIE: (*Giggling.*) Do what you like. You're the one who's worried.

HARRY: (*Coy.*) If I take my things off...will you take yours off?

MARIE: Sod off!

HARRY: (*Mock reluctance.*) I see...okay. You want me to start. You want me to strip first.

MARIE: You suit yourself, lad.

HARRY: I'll do it...just to get some peace...I'll do it. I'll take my things off.

(*HARRY moves centre stage. TIM hums appropriate accompaniment. HARRY does his strip. His movements are slow, very stylised, mock-erotic. First he peels off his sweater and dances around the girls, teasing them with it.*)

MARIE: (*Giggling.*) Look at that pot.

HARRY: (*Sticks out his stomach.*) That is not a pot. That's muscle...in repose.

MARIE: You'll have a dirty big pot before long.

HARRY: And what about you, darling?

(*HARRY slips off his sandals, tosses one to MARIE, one to BELLA.*

BELLA ducks aside. MARIE picks up the sandal and slings it at HARRY. He ducks and it vanishes in the sand. HARRY looks briefly, resumes his strip.

Slowly he unbuckles his belt and dangles it suggestively before MARIE. She giggles and makes a grab for it.)

Naughty! You'll be outa the club.

MARIE: You should be in the clubs.

(*HARRY lowers his jeans to his knees, waggles his pelvis. The girls look away, embarrassed, then look back, giggling.*

HARRY drops his jeans, takes them off, repeats his dance.

He stands posing in string drawers, like Charles Atlas.)

HARRY: Look at that. (*Showing his muscle.*) Just look at that. You too can have a body like mine.

MARIE: I'll stick to me own.

HARRY: You'll go blind.

MARIE: I bet he eats peanut butter.

HARRY: And now...

(*HARRY hooks his hands in his pants. Pause.*)

TIM: (*Shouting.*) Get them down! Get them down!

HARRY: (*To TIM.*) With a roll on the drums and a blast on the trumpet...

(*HARRY slips off the string drawers and twirls them. TIM accompanies with music.*)

MARIE: (*Laughing, looking away and back.*) Dirty bugger!

HARRY: A beauty!

BELLA: Haven't you got a costume?

HARRY: I thought I'd give you a treat.

(*The girls giggle, look away, whisper to each other. HARRY puts on his trunks.*)

All right. Who's on next?

(*HARRY sits down and studies the girls.*)

MARIE: Him.

(*MARIE points to TIM, who turns away.*)

TIM: No.

HARRY: By popular demand...

BELLA: Aren't you getting changed?

TIM: (*Coy.*) I'm not...hot...

BELLA: Go on.

MARIE: He's shy...

TIM: (*Prissy.*) I am *not.*

BELLA: Are you shy?

TIM: (*Hiding his face.*) Shucks...I...gee...

BELLA: Ahh...go on...

HARRY: (*Whisper.*) His...torso...is divine...

(*Pause. Suddenly TIM turns front.*)

TIM: (*Elaborately bashful.*) Ahh...now look...you're not...pulling my...

HARRY: (*Whisper.*) I've never seen another like it.

MARIE: Go on!

BELLA: Yeah...go on...

TIM: Now...you...oh, all right then. But...but promise...

BELLA: What?

TIM: (*Writhing embarrassment.*) You won't...you won't *look* at me...you won't look or anything?

BELLA: Look?

MARIE: We wouldn't *look* at you.

BELLA: Don't be soft.

TIM: I'd feel so...cheap.

MARIE: Go on then.

(*TIM fumbles and tugs at his sweater in a mock paroxysm of nervous modesty. He averts his head, giggles, looks coy, gasps, struggles with his buttons and manages to undo them with incredible slowness...*

MARIE claps ironically.

TIM takes up one of the towels and holds it in front of himself with one hand while with the other he fumbles with

his jeans and eventually slips out of them...
MARIE snatches away the towel.
TIM stands in black briefs and socks, hunching himself up
and crossing his arms to hide his body.)
(*Very appreciative.*) Aye aye aye aye.

BELLA: Sexy kecks.

TIM: (*Very coy.*) They don't...take...much washing.

MARIE: I think they look great.

BELLA: You do look funny in your socks and drawers.
(*TIM whips off his briefs.*)
Dirty bugger!

MARIE: He's as bad as *he* is.

BELLA: They're both the same...

MARIE: Exhibitionists!
(*The girls laugh, glance away, glance back.*)

HARRY: A beauty.

MARIE: Dirty buggers!
(*HARRY claps.*
TIM picks up the towel again and conceals himself with it as,
clumsily, still standing, he takes off his socks and tosses one to
MARIE, one to BELLA. MARIE throws it back.
TIM slips into his trunks and sits down.)
You can get locked up for that.

TIM: Thousands do it every night.

HARRY: (*Pointing at TIM's trunks.*) Watch it, mate.

TIM: What?

HARRY: You're on show. (*Then to MARIE.*) Don't be piping,
now.

MARIE: Who's piping?

TIM: (*Adjusting himself.*) These bloody trunks were designed
for a eunuch.

BELLA: A what?

TIM: A eunuch.

BELLA: What's a eunuch?

TIM: A man without a dick.

BELLA: (*Shocked.*) Oh!

TIM: (*Reassuring.*) Don't worry...I have. (*Pause.*) Are you
coming into the woods now?

BELLA: No thanks.

MARIE: He's in a hurry.

TIM: Don't you want to?

BELLA: (*Laughs.*) I wanna get some suntan.

HARRY: Take your clothes off.

MARIE: He's off again.

HARRY: You're sweating...

MARIE: (*Dry.*) Must be the heat.

HARRY: Don't say I didn't warn you.

MARIE: I'm all right.

(*HARRY takes a bottle of suntan oil from the bag.*)

HARRY: (*To MARIE.*) Oil me.

MARIE: Oil yourself.

HARRY: (*As if surprised.*) Don't you want to oil me?

MARIE: (*Sarcastic.*) Ohhh...I'd get carried away.

HARRY: That's all right as long as you don't spill the oil.

MARIE: Okay.

HARRY: Put plenty on...but spread it.

MARIE: Yes, lover. (*MARIE rubs the oil on HARRY.*)

HARRY: Christ!

MARIE: (*Jumps.*) What?

HARRY: Your nails!

MARIE: Sorry...did I scratch you?

HARRY: You're tearing me to shreds. (*HARRY examines her nails.*)

MARIE: I like them long. Don't you?

HARRY: You certainly do.

MARIE: Don't you?

HARRY: As long as they're not buried in me back.

MARIE: Lie down...

HARRY: (*Lying down.*) Go easy with the talons.

MARIE: (*Rubbing.*) Poor ickle babby...

HARRY: (*Twisting.*) Ooohhhh.

MARIE: Is that nice?

HARRY: Lovely...aaahhh.

MARIE: You're lovely and firm...

HARRY: Do my legs.

(*HARRY lies back while MARIE rubs his legs.*)

MARIE: Ooohhh... Aren't they smooth?

HARRY: (*Prissy.*) They're covered in golden...down.

MARIE: (*Stroking.*) I think they're gorgeous...

HARRY: (*Smug, drawling.*) Of course I look after myself.

MARIE: I bet you do.

HARRY: I'm the athletic type.

MARIE: Yeah?

HARRY: Can't get me off the rugger pitch, you know...

MARIE: No.

HARRY: Up all night with my chest expander...

MARIE: You look after your body...

HARRY: Oh I do indeed. If I look after anything, I look after my body. (*Pause.*) Well...it's the only one I have, you know.

MARIE: Turn...over.

HARRY: (*Turns over.*) Don't forget that.

MARIE: What?

HARRY: (*Points to his trunks.*) That.

MARIE: You can oil that yourself.

HARRY: It's self-lubricating.

MARIE: (*Oiling his thighs.*) Dirty bugger...

HARRY: Ahhhhh.

MARIE: I think he's gonna pass out...

HARRY: It's like a dream...

MARIE: Is it?

HARRY: ...a wet dream...

(*MARIE puts the bottle down.*)

MARIE: You can oil yourself.

HARRY: Sorry...go on...

MARIE: You gonna behave?

HARRY: (*Childish.*) Promise to be a good boy.

MARIE: All right.

HARRY: Do me back.

(*HARRY lies on his stomach while MARIE oils his back.*)

MARIE: You're nice and brown already.

HARRY: Don't forget my legs.

MARIE: I won't.

HARRY: Easy...that's sensitive.

MARIE: Sorry...is that all right?

HARRY: Lovely.

(*MARIE strokes the back of his legs, and his thighs.*)

Ahhhhh.

MARIE: All right?

HARRY: (*Twisting.*) Ahhhh...aaaahhhhhh.

MARIE: (*Laughing.*) I think he's in for a fit.

HARRY: AAAHHHHHHHH.

(*HARRY slumps. MARIE jumps.*)

MARIE: What's the matter?

HARRY: (*Groaning.*) Ooohhh.

MARIE: Are you all right?

HARRY: Mmmmmm.

MARIE: What happened?

HARRY: (*Faint.*) Eh?

MARIE: (*Grinning.*) What happened then...?

HARRY: I shot me load.

MARIE: (*Howls with laughter.*) YOU WHAT?

HARRY: (*Weak.*) I shot me load.

MARIE: What's that?

BELLA: He what?

HARRY: Ask your mam.

TIM: He was foaming at the thighs.

MARIE: (*Laughing.*) Dirty bugger!

HARRY: I'll be all right in twenty-seven minutes.

MARIE: All right.

HARRY: I'll be ready by then.

MARIE: (*Grinning.*) Ready for what?

HARRY: A bit of the other.

MARIE: You can...sod off!

(*HARRY lies back, stretches luxuriously.*)

HARRY: (*Deep drawl.*) God...what a super morning. I'm positive it's going to be an absolutely super day. Isn't the sky absolutely super? I think I'll have a little shut-eye...build up my strength for later, darling.

(*MARIE lies near BELLA.*)

MARIE: Keep your eye on him, Bella.

HARRY: Aren't you going to put any oil on yourself?

MARIE: I'm all right.

HARRY: You won't be for long. You'd better put some on or you'll frizzle.

(*MARIE dabs some oil on her face and arms. Then she dabs her stockings.*)

Christ!

MARIE: What?

HARRY: Why don't you take them off?

MARIE: You go asleep.

HARRY: Nobody's gonna stare at you.

TIM: You speak for yourself.

(*Pause. HARRY sits up, stares at MARIE.*)

MARIE: What are you looking at?

HARRY: You could always go and get changed in the woods.

MARIE: Changed?

HARRY: You might just as well.

MARIE: Haven't got a costume.

(*Pause.*)

HARRY: I said we'd be coming to the beach.

MARIE: Huh.

HARRY: Why didn't you bring a costume?

MARIE: (*Emphatic.*) I haven't *got* a costume.

HARRY: You haven't *got* a costume?

MARIE: I told you.

HARRY: (*Edgy.*) Couldn't you borrow your grannie's or something?

MARIE: Me grannie hasn't got one either.

HARRY: Christ! (*Pause. To BELLA.*) What about you?

BELLA: What?

HARRY: Have you?

(*BELLA shakes her head. HARRY looks at TIM, then at the girls.*)

You're gonna melt away here when the sun gets up.

MARIE: Well…you're all right. You've got yours.

HARRY: You'd be better off in bra and pants.

MARIE: Aye aye!

HARRY: You'd probably be better covered than in a costume.

MARIE: We'll be okay. (*Pause.*)

TIM: See how you feel after…

> (*TIM oils himself. BELLA watches. HARRY and MARIE are lying back.*)

BELLA: Does that make you go brown?

TIM: The oil? It helps. Mainly it stops you going sore.

BELLA: I never go brown.

TIM: Put some of this on.

> (*BELLA dabs herself with the oil.*)

You better put plenty on. You need it with a pale skin…

BELLA: How did you get so brown?

TIM: From me dad…Abdul.

BELLA: Honest…I never go brown.

TIM: What do you go?

BELLA: Pink and horrible.

TIM: Never mind…today you'll go brown and beautiful.

BELLA: Some hope.

> (*BELLA dabs her stockings as MARIE did. TIM watches.*)

TIM: You go brown more quickly if you go in the water.

BELLA: I can't swim.

TIM: You can paddle.

BELLA: And get soaked.

TIM: Take your clothes off.

MARIE: Aye aye aye aye!

BELLA: Can you swim?

TIM: Like an eel.

BELLA: Can you?

TIM: Want me to teach you?

MARIE: Aye aye aye aye!

TIM: Come on…I'll show you…

BELLA: I'm not going in.

TIM: You don't have to go in.

BELLA: I'm dead beat.

TIM: Come on… (*He stands and takes her hand.*)

BELLA: Honest… I'm aching…

TIM: This'll revive you.

MARIE: I bet it will!

BELLA: You only just put the oil on.

TIM: I'll show you the movements…
MARIE: Aye aye aye aye!
TIM: (*Prissy.*) She's only jealous.
BELLA: (*Rising.*) I dunno…
HARRY: (*Solicitous.*) Will you be okay, mate?
TIM: I guess so.
HARRY: Want me to come with you?
TIM: I'll shout if I get into trouble.
HARRY: Don't let yourself get carried away, now.
TIM: Will you be all right here?

(*TIM glances sideways at MARIE.*)

MARIE: Cheeky sod!
HARRY: (*Brave.*) Don't worry about me.
TIM: I'll be listening.
HARRY: (*Prissy.*) Oh, will you?

(*TIM picks up the beachball and throws it to BELLA.*)

TIM: Catch.

(*BELLA misses it.*)

Butterfingers!

(*BELLA picks up the ball and hits TIM with it as he stoops.*)

BELLA: Catch. (*She laughs.*)

(*BELLA runs off. TIM picks up the ball, follows.*
*Sound of shouting for a moment, then silence. MARIE goes to
the top of the dune and looks down. Then she comes back and
sits by HARRY, who is lying on his back with his eyes closed.
She looks at him. After a while she fiddles with the transistor.
She eats another orange and takes a swig of the lemonade.*
HARRY opens his eyes.)

HARRY: I wish you'd shut up and let's have a kip.
MARIE: (*Laughing.*) Kip off!

(*MARIE stretches out on the other side of the blanket.*)

HARRY: Sweet dreams.

(*Pause. The transistor is very loud. MARIE lies on her back
with her eyes closed. HARRY sits up and scrutinizes her, then
lies back. After a moment he sits up again, restlessly, and
again looks MARIE up and down.*
He takes a sip of lemonade.)

Then he goes to the top of the dune and looks around. Comes back down and lies next to MARIE.
He takes her hand.
She moves her hand away.
He lowers the transistor, lies back. After a minute of silence he begins to whistle and snore, at first quietly, then wildly and loudly.)

MARIE: (*Laughing.*) Jesus!

HARRY: Go asleep.

MARIE: I'm trying to go asleep.

HARRY: You keep waking me up just when I'm drifting off.

MARIE: Oh, I'm sorry.

(*They close their eyes. After a silence, HARRY resumes frantic whistling and snoring.*)

Christ!

HARRY: What's the matter?

MARIE: Ever tried sleeping on your side?

HARRY: (*Drawls.*) What a super idea.

(*HARRY turns on his side, now facing MARIE, very close to her.*)

MARIE: Hey up!

(*MARIE edges away a little.*)

HARRY: You're off the blanket.

MARIE: I'm all right…

HARRY: Lie on the blanket…you'll get fulla sand.

MARIE: (*Moving nearer.*) I'm all right now…

HARRY: (*Pulling her nearer.*) You're not properly on…

MARIE: I'm all right now.

(*HARRY reaches across her, tugs the blanket, and then pulls MARIE toward him. He tries to kiss her.*)

(*Pushing back.*) Sod *off!*

HARRY: (*Sincere tone.*) All I want is some sex off you.

MARIE: (*Laughing.*) Cheeky bugger!

(*MARIE pushes him away, and lies back, with her eyes closed. HARRY looks at her legs, then leans forward and moans.*)

What are you doing now?

HARRY: Looking up your frock.

MARIE: Bugger!

(*MARIE pulls her skirt tight around her legs.*)

HARRY: (*Mock-peevish.*) Oh you...spoilsport!

MARIE: Shouldn't be peeping.

HARRY: I wasn't peeping...I was staring. (*Pause.*) You've got lovely legs. I like to look up them.

MARIE: (*Dry.*) Oh...thanks very much.

HARRY: Now I can't see a thing.

(*HARRY slides back alongside her and stares at her neck and sweater.*)

MARIE: Gerroff!

HARRY: I can just see the top of your bra.

MARIE: Can you?

HARRY: (*Drawls.*) Makes me feel quite horny, really.

MARIE: You make me feel naked.

HARRY: (*Brightly.*) Why not strip off?

MARIE: Aye aye!

HARRY: You'll feel better.

MARIE: I wanna have a doze...

HARRY: Go on...

MARIE: Are you gonna behave?

HARRY: Go on...you have a doze...

MARIE: I feel as if I could drop right off.

HARRY: (*Leering.*) I'll watch over you, darling.

MARIE: (*Laughing.*) Oh sure!

HARRY: Go on...

MARIE: You lie down there...

(*MARIE points to a spot alongside her on the blanket. HARRY lies down, very obediently.*)

HARRY: Here?

MARIE: Yeah.

(*MARIE closes her eyes.*

HARRY closes his.

After a moment he begins to stroke his foot against hers.)
Stop it. You're tickling.

HARRY: (*Prissy.*) Oh I'm sorry about that.

MARIE: Go asleep.

(*HARRY lies back. Then he sits up again, plucks a blade of grass and begins tickling her face with it.*)

SHUH!

HARRY: Did that tickle?

MARIE: Lay off...I'm dead beat.

HARRY: Close your eyes...

(*MARIE closes her eyes.*
HARRY leans forward with his face only inches from hers.
After a moment she opens her eyes and jumps.)

MARIE: OH!

HARRY: Relax...

MARIE: With two blue big eyes staring into me...?

HARRY: (*Very intense tone.*) You know...you're lovely.

MARIE: (*Smiling.*) Oh aye...

HARRY: Is your hair dyed?

MARIE: No...it's genuine red.

HARRY: I love you.

MARIE: (*Surprised, smiling.*) Eh?

HARRY: (*Urgent.*) Give us a kiss.

(*He kisses her cheeks, lightly. She turns her face away.*)

MARIE: Gerroff!

HARRY: (*Mock-surprise.*) Don't *you* love me?

MARIE: Oh aye!

HARRY: (*Smug.*) Madly?

MARIE: Oh aye...ever since I first saw you.

HARRY: (*Smug.*) That's what they all say.

MARIE: Conceited sod.

HARRY: I'm absolutely crazy about you.

MARIE: Are you, lad?

HARRY: I love you...

MARIE: (*Laughs.*) Do you?

HARRY: (*Ardent.*) Yeah.

MARIE: Forever?

HARRY: Forever now.

MARIE: (*Pushing him.*) Gerroff...you're all sweaty.

HARRY: (*Groaning.*) I'm burning with lust!

MARIE: You better go and see your mate.

HARRY: Give us a kiss.

(*They kiss lightly, then more urgently.*)

MARIE: Your face is all sandy.

HARRY: Wipe it off.

(*MARIE wipes the sand off. They lie close.*)

Listen.

MARIE: What?

HARRY: Can't you hear it?

MARIE: Hear what?

HARRY: Close your eyes and listen.

(*MARIE closes her eyes. HARRY sits up, looking at her.*)

MARIE: I can't hear anything.

HARRY: Concentrate.

(*HARRY lifts her skirt to her waist. She jumps away, annoyed but giggling.*)

Listen. The tide's coming in.

MARIE: Dirty bugger!

HARRY: (*Injured.*) I only wanted to look at your legs.

MARIE: Lay off.

HARRY: (*Pleading.*) Go on…

MARIE: Sod off!

HARRY: Lend us a feel till Friday.

MARIE: Feel yourself.

HARRY: Come here.

(*MARIE sits facing him.*)

(*Coy.*) Do you fancy a bit?

MARIE: I fancy a bit of peace.

HARRY: Let's go and lie down.

MARIE: Lie down where?

HARRY: Over there. It's too hot here.

MARIE: Over where?

(*HARRY kisses her passionately. He half rises, takes her hand.*)

HARRY: Come on.

MARIE: (*Resisting.*) Where are we going?

HARRY: Over there…the trees.

MARIE: Let's stay here.

HARRY: It's too hot.

MARIE: You're too hot.

HARRY: We can lie down in the shade.

MARIE: No…come here. (*MARIE kisses him.*)

HARRY: What's the matter?

MARIE: Nothing.

HARRY: Let's go and lie in the shade…

MARIE: Maybe *they're* in the shade now…

HARRY: Well…we'll share the shade.

MARIE: Nooo…

HARRY: Why?

(*MARIE kisses him. Smiles at him. HARRY looks at her. Holds her hand. Silence.*)

MARIE: You've got nice eyes.

HARRY: I won't rape you.

MARIE: Oh well I won't go.

HARRY: (*Laughs.*) Come on…

MARIE: You don't give up…

HARRY: Don't you trust me?

MARIE: (*Giggling.*) I trust you…

HARRY: What?

MARIE: I don't trust myself.

(*HARRY lies beside her. He touches her sweater. She puts her hand over his.*
He tries to slip his hand underneath but she stops him. They stay locked for a moment.)
NO!

HARRY: I only want to feel your tits.

MARIE: Somehow I guessed.

HARRY: It's all right.

MARIE: What?

HARRY: What's wrong?

MARIE: Nothing.

HARRY: You're very well built.

MARIE: Somebody'll come.

HARRY: Let's go over there…

MARIE: No.

(*HARRY tugs her, teasingly. MARIE pulls away.*
He falls on her and they wrestle. MARIE grabs his hands.)
Lay off!
(*HARRY presses her down with his weight and bites her neck. She struggles but is trapped.*)
OW!

HARRY: (*Biting.*) Mmmmmmm.
MARIE: *Stop biting!* Ow! BUGGER!
  (*HARRY frees her and she squints to see the bite.*)
HARRY: (*Proud.*) That'll really come up.
MARIE: That hurt like hell.
HARRY: You're branded.
MARIE: Can you see it over the sweater?
HARRY: Oh yes.
MARIE: (*Adjusting the sweater.*) Can you?
HARRY: A dirty big red lovebite.
MARIE: (*Giggling.*) You bastard. (*She slaps him lightly.*)
  (*HARRY pushes her down again.*)
HARRY: Let's go into the woods.
MARIE: You go.
HARRY: I'll eat you all up.
  (*HARRY bites her again.*)
MARIE: I'll scratch.
  (*HARRY ignores her.*
  She scratches his cheek and he jumps back.)
HARRY: OW! BITCH!
MARIE: (*Pleased.*) I *warned* you.
HARRY: (*Squinting.*) Does it look bad?
MARIE: It's bleeding.
HARRY: Lick it.
MARIE: Gerroff!
HARRY: Lick it.
  (*HARRY shoves his face towards hers and they wrestle. BELLA
  comes to the top of the dune and watches, casually.*
  HARRY sees her and frees a hand to wave. They wrestle.
  MARIE sees BELLA.)
MARIE: Help! Bella...get this bugger off. He's eating me.
BELLA: (*Coming down.*) Who's eating who?
HARRY: I've been assaulted.
  (*The girls push HARRY away. He lies back on the blanket.*)
  Thanks, Bella. You were just in time.
BELLA: For what?
HARRY: She was tearing me to bits.
MARIE: Bugger!

BELLA: They're both as bad.

HARRY: What?

MARIE: Eh?

BELLA: Him...and his mate. (*Pause.*)

HARRY: (*Tough guy tone.*) I hope you haven't...done anything...to my mate...

BELLA: I left him tied to a tree.

HARRY: Poor Tim.

BELLA: (*Laughs.*) I think he'll live.

MARIE: (*Showing the bites.*) Look what this bastard did to me.

BELLA: Look at this.

(*BELLA points to her own bites.*
The girls compare.)

MARIE: Think it'll show tomorrow?

BELLA: Looks like.

MARIE: The bastard...I bet it'll go all purple.

BELLA: Do you think this'll show?

MARIE: Let's see...

BELLA: He didn't half hurt...

MARIE: Very nasty.

BELLA: Its gonna turn into a real bruise...

MARIE: What'll they say in work?

BELLA: You'll have to wear a high neck.

HARRY: (*Prissy.*) And what about me with me face torn to bits? I daren't face me friends. What'll all the fellers say?

MARIE: You came back just in time, Bel.

BELLA: I was waiting over there.

HARRY: (*Mock indignant.*) Spying on us.

(*TIM enters. He struggles toward HARRY.*)

TIM: (*Choked voice.*) Gawd...

HARRY: (*High-pitched.*) Tim!

TIM: Harry!

HARRY: You...made it back...

TIM: It's good to see you...mate...

HARRY: You made it back.

TIM: Shucks...

HARRY: Was it...rough?

TIM: (*Turns away.*) I'd rather not...talk about it.

HARRY: No...no. (*Pause.*) Was it rough?

TIM: Ahhhhhhh.

HARRY: Are you all right?

TIM: (*Choked.*) Don't worry...about...me.

HARRY: I understand.

TIM: One thing...

HARRY: What? What?

TIM: One thing I want to ask you...

HARRY: Anything.

(*The two men stare intently at each other, ignoring the girls completely. The girls stare intently at the men.*)

What?

TIM: I realize I have no right to ask this...

HARRY: Ask me. Ask me anything.

(*Pause.*)

TIM: Did you get your hole?

HARRY: No. (*Pause.*) Did you?

TIM: No.

(*The men look commiseratingly at each other.*)

Never mind... mate.

HARRY: Not worth torturing yourself...

TIM: You know what they are.

HARRY: They're just... (*Waves his hand.*)

TIM: They're just a couple of prickteasers.

HARRY: That's it.

MARIE: You what?

HARRY: That's what they are...

TIM: Prickteasers.

MARIE: What?

BELLA: Prickwhat?

HARRY: PRICK-TEASERS!

(*Both girls have a fit of giggling and laughing.*)

MARIE: Dirty buggers!

BELLA: Prickteasers!

MARIE: They use some lovely language.

BELLA: Cheeky buggers!

MARIE: (*Convulsed.*) Prickteasers!

(*The men lie down on the blanket.*)

TIM: Gawd... I'm exhausted.

HARRY: Have a kip. I'll keep watch.

MARIE: (*To BELLA.*) You all right?

BELLA: Just about.

MARIE: Did you learn to swim?

BELLA: HA HA.

HARRY: (*To TIM.*) Have a buttie.

TIM: Thanks. Are you having one?

HARRY: I'm having an orange.

> (*The girls suddenly look at each other and go off into a fit of giggling again.*)

MARIE: I'm going over there...

BELLA: Oh.

MARIE: Are you gonna hold my hand?

BELLA: Yeah...I'll come with you.

> (*They head off towards the woods, still giggling.*)

HARRY: Where are you going?

MARIE: For a piss.

> (*The girls exit.*)

HARRY: (*Queer tone.*) FOR A PISS!

> (*HARRY and TIM sit looking at each other.*
> *Silence. HARRY jumps up to the top of the dune.*)
> (*Laughs.*) And the waters covered the earth...
> (*He comes down and lies by TIM.*
> *Silence.*)

TIM: Jesus!

HARRY: Yeah...

TIM: What time is it?

HARRY: About ten o'clock.

TIM: Only ten o'clock...

HARRY: I know... (*Silence.*)

TIM: The state of them.

HARRY: Notice what they're wearing?

TIM: Same as last night.

HARRY: Exactly.

TIM: Wait till the sun gets up.

HARRY: (*Holding his nose.*) Ugggghhh.

TIM: It's gonna be a scorcher, too. (*Silence.*)

HARRY: All they did was put fresh paint on.

TIM: The van stunk this morning.

HARRY: I had the fan on.

TIM: Yeah...it was blowing a gale.

HARRY: The stuff they put on.

TIM: No wonder they give off.

HARRY: What a bloody pong.

TIM: It's the sweat.

HARRY: And the rest...

    (*Silence.*)

TIM: (*Wry laugh.*) Last night was great.

HARRY: That was in the alehouse...

TIM: And after...

HARRY: We musta been pissed.

TIM: Seemed different then. (*Silence.*)

HARRY: (*Laughs.*) We'll have to stay in the friggin' water.

TIM: (*Laughs.*) What...all day?

HARRY: We said we'd take them for a drink afterwards, too.

TIM: Yeah.

HARRY: Maybe we could go early...

TIM: How?

HARRY: Say it's to avoid the traffic?

TIM: How early?

HARRY: I dunno...four o'clock.

TIM: Another six hours.

HARRY: Jesus!

    (*Silence.*

    TIM stares at HARRY, and slowly begins to grin, then chuckle.

    HARRY responds.)

    What a fucking stink.

TIM: Lovely!

HARRY: Lovely!

    (*Both men lie back, laughing, holding their noses. The girls shout in the distance.*

    TIM gets up quickly.)

TIM: Come on...

HARRY: What?

TIM: (*Queer tone.*) D'you wanna go for a piss?
HARRY: (*Queer tone.*) Can I hold your hand?
TIM: Come on...they'll be back in a minute.
HARRY: (*Joins him.*) Right.
TIM: (*Laughing.*) The dirty cows!
HARRY: (*Laughing.*) The dirty cows!
   (*They run off toward the beach.*
   Sound of the girls' voices, and pop music.)

   Curtain.

ACT TWO

About midday. The girls lie on the blanket, MARIE reading a paperback, BELLA dozing. The transistor is playing. MARIE is very restless. She puts the paperback down.

MARIE: Dirty buggers!
   (*BELLA doesn't respond. MARIE takes an orange from the bag. Swigs some lemonade. Looks at what is left in the bottle, puts the bottle back. She peels the orange, tosses the peel aside. Eats the orange. Her hands are sticky, so she rubs them on her skirt. Spits out pips.*
   She gets up, spins round to the music, turns up the volume. Then she goes to the top of the dune and looks across toward the beach.
   After a minute she comes back down. Another little shake to the music. She sits down, stares at BELLA. She leans across and taps her.)
BELLA: (*Stirring.*) Ehhh?
MARIE: You wanna orange?
BELLA: Oh...ta... No, I'll have a drink. (*BELLA takes out the bottle.*)
MARIE: Go easy...there's not much left.
BELLA: No...you've been swigging it all morning.
MARIE: Well...
BELLA: You have.
MARIE: (*Snaps.*) There's sod all else to do.
   (*BELLA sips, puts the bottle back.*)
BELLA: Have a sleep.
MARIE: I've had a sleep.
BELLA: Don't pick on me.
MARIE: What time is it?
BELLA: I dunno.
MARIE: Feels like we been here all bloody summer.
BELLA: Am I brown?
MARIE: Oh you're lovely... (*BELLA dabs on some oil.*)
   They're taking their time.
BELLA: They musta gone for a swim.

MARIE: Wish I could swim...hey...shall we go down?

BELLA: Down where?

MARIE: Down there...to the beach?

BELLA: You go.

MARIE: Oh aye...

(*MARIE goes to the top of the dune.*)

BELLA: Can you see them?

MARIE: No.

BELLA Maybe they swam out.

MARIE: Yea...over to New Brighton, probably!

BELLA: Come down.

MARIE: There's no sign of them...

(*BELLA puts the oil away, stretches, and sprawls on her back on the blanket.*)

BELLA: They'll be back...come down.

(*MARIE comes down and throws herself on to the blanket. She picks up the book. Her eyes widen.*)

MARIE: This book...it's crazy.

BELLA: Is it?

MARIE: Yeah...it's... (*She tosses it aside. Pause.*)

BELLA: Huh?

MARIE: Do you fancy him?

BELLA: Who?

MARIE: Santa Claus! (*Silence.*) Who do you think?

BELLA: Oh...he's all right.

MARIE: He musta been all right last night.

BELLA: (*Grinning.*) How do you mean?

MARIE: In the backa the van.

BELLA: He was all right.

(*Pause.*)

MARIE: (*Laughs.*) Did you get your hole?

BELLA: (*Laughs.*) You mean, did he get his?

MARIE: Dirty buggers! (*Pause.*)

BELLA: Anyway...you were doing all right yourself...

MARIE: Eh?

BELLA: In the front of the van.

MARIE: (*Grinning.*) Oh aye...

BELLA: They don't waste much time...

MARIE: They didn't last night...but...

BELLA: Yeah...

MARIE: I bet they've had some fun out here.

BELLA: After Saturday night.

MARIE: What?

BELLA: If they pick anything up on Saturday night.

MARIE: Oh yeah... Cheeky sod! (*Pause.*)

BELLA: That bite's going blue.

MARIE: Is it? (*Squinting.*)

BELLA: Tomorrow it'll be all purple.

MARIE: What about yours?

BELLA: (*Squints.*) Yeah... (*Pulls up her sweater.*) But look at this one.

MARIE: Jesus! You wanna be careful.

BELLA: What?

MARIE: He'll bite it off.

BELLA: (*Laughing.*) Wants his mammy.

MARIE: You musta got him real worked up.

BELLA: Doesn't take much.

MARIE: (*Howls with laughter.*) Prickteaser!

BELLA: (*Laughing.*) Prickteaser!

(*Both girls double up on the blanket in a fit of laughing and giggling.*
They lie back.)

Christ...it's hot.

MARIE: Yeah...

BELLA: Wish we had costumes.

MARIE: Yeah...I'm melting away.

BELLA: I'd give anything for a pan of cold water.

MARIE: Yeah...the sand sticks to you.

BELLA: I'm soaked in sweat.

MARIE: Me too.

(*MARIE gets her bag, takes out some perfume, dabs herself.*)
That's better. Want some?

BELLA: Ta.

(*BELLA dabs on some perfume.*
MARIE studies herself in a mirror, puts on some make-up.
BELLA watches her, then picks up her own bag and does the same.)

MARIE: Do I look all right?

BELLA: Dead sexy.

MARIE: Oh aye!

BELLA: You look all right.

MARIE: My hair's rotten with sand. (*Scratching.*)

BELLA: (*Looking in the mirror.*) Does that look all right?

MARIE: It's a bit streaky.

BELLA: Yeah… I thought it was.

(*BELLA touches up her make-up.*)

MARIE: That looks better now.

(*Suddenly the beach ball bounces into the middle of the hollow. Both girls jump back. HARRY appears at the top of the dune, stands for a moment, grinning, then leaps down. Fresh from the swim, he stands between the girls, shaking himself and showering them.*)

Sod off!

HARRY: Thought that would cool you down.

(*HARRY dries himself, rubbing vigorously, flexing his muscles.*)

MARIE: How was New Brighton?

HARRY: Eh? Oh…too crowded to stay.

MARIE: Thought you'd got drowned.

HARRY: Worried about your lift home?

BELLA: Where's your mate?

HARRY: In the woods.

BELLA: (*Laughing.*) He wastes not time, does he? (*Gets up.*)

I'll go and see what he's up to.

HARRY: I'll tell you if you really want to know.

(*BELLA goes off left.*

HARRY sits down, looks in the beach bag.)

Where's all the oranges?

MARIE: (*Points to peelings.*) There.

HARRY: Christ…

MARIE: We were dying of thirst.

HARRY: What about the lemonade? (*Examines the bottle.*)

You might just as well have finished it off.

MARIE: I will if you like.

HARRY: I believe you.

MARIE: There's some butties left.

HARRY: Thanks very much!

(HARRY takes a sip of the lemonade and eats a sandwich.)

MARIE: There was sod all to do.

HARRY: Huh.

MARIE: You were gone ages.

HARRY: We had a good swim.

MARIE: Wish I could swim.

HARRY: You shoulda brought a costume.

MARIE: I haven't got a costume.

(Pause. HARRY eats his sandwich. Fiddles with the transistor.)

HARRY: *(Sourly.)* WONDERFUL RADIO ONE!

MARIE: What's the matter with it?

HARRY: That's the fifteenth time the DJ's played that brand new number. He must puke whenever he puts it on.

(Pause.) It's okay once, but fifteen times!

MARIE: It hasn't been on fifteen times.

HARRY: Well, ten times, seven times, whatever it is. Maybe that's why they keep changing the DJs – because they don't change the tunes.

(HARRY finishes the sandwich, licks his lips.)

Now it's my turn to die of thirst.

MARIE: *(Leaning toward him.)* I'll give you a big sloppy kiss…that'll help your thirst.

HARRY: What? A mouthful of spit?

MARIE: It's nice.

HARRY: I'd rather suck me thumb. *(HARRY sits sucking his thumb.)*

MARIE: Poor little baby. *(HARRY – sucking sounds.)*

(Pushing her breasts out.) Wanna drop of milk?

HARRY: I only drink sterilized. *(They sit for a moment.)*

(BELLA returns.)

MARIE: Where is he?

BELLA: In the woods.

MARIE: Did you find him?

BELLA: Yeah.

(BELLA sits. She looks at HARRY.)

What's he doing?

MARIE: Sucking his thumb. *(Pause.)* Where is he then?

BELLA: He was sitting under a tree.

MARIE: Oh.

BELLA: I asked him what he was doing. He just looked at me. So I came back.

HARRY: He was probably having a crap.

BELLA: With his costume on?

HARRY: He's very modest. (*Pause.*)

MARIE: Whose is the book?

HARRY: What book?

MARIE: This one...it was in the van.

HARRY: Somebody musta left it in the van.

MARIE: Wonder who?

HARRY: Have you read it?

MARIE: Bits of it.

HARRY: Like it?

MARIE: (*Giggles*) It's a scream.

HARRY: (*Indignant tone.*) It's a well-known Indian sex manual.

MARIE: Yeah...a dirty book.

HARRY: What's dirty about it?

MARIE: I prefer sex the English way.

HARRY: Christ...a patriot!

(*TIM returns and sits by HARRY.*)

TIM: Pass us an orange.

HARRY: It's the last one.

TIM: I'll give you a slice.

(*HARRY passes the orange.*)

Any lemonade?

HARRY: Just a drop.

(*HARRY passes the lemonade. TIM drains it.*)

MARIE: Shoulda brought some more.

TIM: (*To HARRY.*) How much did you have?

HARRY: Just a swig.

TIM: So did I.

HARRY: We had three bottles this morning.

TIM: How many oranges did you have?

HARRY: Two.

TIM: I only had one.

MARIE: You had two.

TIM: You had ten.

MARIE: I was thirsty.

TIM: Greedy cow!

HARRY: You've been at it all day.

MARIE: What do you want me to do? Run and fetch some more?

TIM: Any butties left?

HARRY: No. All gone.

MARIE: You had your share.

TIM: I'm dying for a drink.

(*Pause.*)

HARRY: D'you wanna go…get a drink on the way?

(*Pause.*)

MARIE: What time is it?

HARRY: About half twelve.

MARIE: It's early.

TIM: Pubs'll be open till two.

MARIE: You mean go and come back?

TIM: Could do…

HARRY: Not much time…

TIM: Gorta get away early, though…avoid the jams.

HARRY: Yeah.

(*Silence.*)

BELLA: I wanna get some tan in.

MARIE: Yeah.

BELLA: (*To TIM.*) Am I brown?

TIM: You're all pink and horrible.

BELLA: Thanks very much!

TIM: You said you would be.

BELLA: You said I wouldn't.

TIM: (*Wry.*) Wrong again.

(*BELLA grimaces, lies back. TIM does the same. Pause. MARIE takes a blade of grass and traces it across HARRY's face.*)

MARIE: You wore out?

HARRY: Yeah.

MARIE: It's the sun.

HARRY: Huh.

MARIE: Wanna go in the shade?

HARRY: I wanna go asleep.

MARIE: You could go asleep…

HARRY: Oh yeah…

    (*MARIE climbs to the top of the dune, looks around, comes back to HARRY.*)

MARIE: Like a desert island.

HARRY: Waiting for a ship.

MARIE: Yeah. (*Pause.*) Is this where you come to do your courting?

HARRY: No, this is where we come to do our fucking.

MARIE: (*Laughs.*) You coulda fooled me.

HARRY: We do our courting in the alehouse.

MARIE: Like last night?

HARRY: That's right.

MARIE: Where?

HARRY: Eh?

MARIE: D'you go in the woods?

HARRY: They're fulla flies and dogshit.

    (*HARRY turns and lies on his stomach with his eyes closed.*)

MARIE: Ooohhh…look at all the little curly hairs sticking out.

HARRY: Bugger off.

    (*MARIE pats him. Plucks a hair. HARRY jumps.*)
    OW!

MARIE: Big baby.

HARRY: (*Twists away.*) Lay off.

    (*MARIE fiddles with the transistor.*)

MARIE: Let's have a dance… (*She stands dancing by herself.*)

HARRY: You have a dance.

MARIE: Come on…

HARRY: I'm too tired.

MARIE: Go asleep then.

HARRY: I'm trying…I'm trying.

    (*MARIE throws a towel over his head. He lets it lie there.*)

MARIE: (*To BELLA.*) How's lover boy?

BELLA: Flaked out.

MARIE: Let's have a dance.

BELLA: Make a change.

(*MARIE turns the transistor full blast, and the girls dance. MARIE kicks the towel away from HARRY. They dance across the men.*)

MARIE: They can't dance.

BELLA: No?

MARIE: Only with each other.

BELLA: Probably.

MARIE: I wonder who leads.

(*The girls laugh and giggle.*)

Christ...I'm sweating.

BELLA: (*Wriggling.*) So am I...soaked.

MARIE: Just think...we coulda been dancing at the Cavern now instead of the bloody sandhills.

BELLA: Yeah.

MARIE: See the talent.

BELLA: Yeah.

MARIE: Mind you, we'd probably be sweating worse.

BELLA: I wouldn't mind.

MARIE: Me neither.

(*MARIE kicks sand over HARRY.*)

HARRY: Bugger you!

MARIE: Jesus, it's alive!

(*The girls lie down.*)

BELLA: (*Pulling at her pants.*) The sand gets in everything.

MARIE: It's a menace.

BELLA: It's all right for them.

HARRY: You shoulda brought costumes.

MARIE: I'd rather go to New Brighton Baths.

HARRY: HAHAHA!

MARIE: What are you laughing at?

HARRY: When did you ever go to the baths?

MARIE: I've been there often.

HARRY: Prefer that, do you?

MARIE: Yeah. (*Then ignoring him, turns to BELLA.*) You can have more laughs at the baths, anyway.

BELLA: You can have more laughs at the morgue!

MARIE: Bloody right.

(*Pause. BELLA leans back. MARIE looks round, restless. Strokes the sand with her hand. She tries to pile it up.*)
(*Childish.*) You can't even build a bloody sandcastle...the sand's no good.

BELLA: The sand's too fine.

(*Long pause. MARIE filters the sand through her fingers. BELLA watches. The men lie with eyes closed. The sun belts down. The transistor is off. Distant sound of ships' sirens.*)

MARIE: (*Looking at the men.*) Look at them...the ravers.

BELLA: Huh...the jet set.

MARIE: Big build-up.

BELLA: Mouth.

MARIE: All mouth.

BELLA: Can't half talk.

MARIE: Yeah.

BELLA: We'll have to find somewhere else to drink.

MARIE: Plenty of places.

BELLA: Start next week.

MARIE: Yeah. (*Pause.*) Mind you...I think these were in the wrong pub.

BELLA: Got mis-directed?

MARIE: (*Laughs.*) Lost their way. (*Pause. Mimicking.*) Passssss ussss an orange.

BELLA: (*Mimicking.*) Ssssave ussss a ssslice.

MARIE: Wonder who's the giver?

(*Both girls burst out laughing.*)

No...you know what they are really?

BELLA: Go on...

MARIE: A couple of...cunt-teasers.

BELLA: (*Laughing.*) Cunt-teasers?

MARIE: You know...a couple of cunt-teasers. (*The girls fall about laughing. HARRY looks at them.*) Know what you are? Cunt-teasers!

HARRY: You should know.

MARIE: Eh.

HARRY: I bet yours has got cobwebs on it.

MARIE: If I waited for you!

(*Both girls howl and roll about laughing. HARRY stares and then slings the beach ball at MARIE. She hurls it back at*

*him. It bounces away. BELLA picks it up. Throws it to
MARIE. MARIE throws it back. BELLA punches it back,
wide. MARIE collects it, comes behind HARRY, bounces the
ball on his stomach.)*

Come on.

HARRY: Eh?

MARIE: You gonna play?

HARRY: Frig off!

MARIE: Thought you was the athletic type?

HARRY: (*Pointing at her breasts.*) Where did you get them?
Outa the catalogue?

MARIE: (*Laughing, bouncing.*) They're all meat, lad.

*(MARIE throws the ball to BELLA. The girls jump around,
across the men, the pace getting faster.*
*MARIE stops, peels off her stockings, flourishes them and
tosses them over HARRY.)*

HARRY: (*Disgusted.*) Bitch!

*(HARRY flings the stockings aside, rolls away. BELLA takes
off her stockings, throws them at TIM. He rolls away. MARIE
hitches her skirt at her waist. BELLA does the same.*
*MARIE feints to hurl the ball at HARRY. He flinches. She
howls with laughter, tosses the ball to BELLA. The girls
leap around, now slinging the ball at each other.*
*MARIE throws the ball at HARRY and catches him hard on
the face. He yelps.)*

OW! BITCH!

MARIE: (*Laughing.*) Oh! Very sorry!

*(The ball bounces off toward TIM. He tries to grab it but
BELLA intercepts it. TIM tackles her, but she avoids him
and tosses it to MARIE. HARRY grabs it, feints to throw it to
TIM but swivels and slings it hard at MARIE. She ducks
and the ball bounces and flies off toward the woods.*
Pause.
*TIM and BELLA stand transfixed on the left, nearer the
woods. Centre stands MARIE. HARRY stands, slightly higher,
on the slope, on the right.*
*MARIE turns round, looks at BELLA, turns back to face
HARRY.*
Silence.)

HARRY: Fetch it.

MARIE: You threw it.

HARRY: At you.

MARIE: Huh!

> (*Pause.*)

HARRY: Fetch it.

MARIE: Sod off! (*Pause.*)

> (*BELLA turns towards the woods, TIM seizes her.*)

BELLA: (*Struggling.*) Leggo.

TIM: Stay there.

BELLA: I'll fetch it.

TIM: You won't.

> (*HARRY comes down toward MARIE.*)

HARRY: Fetch it.

MARIE: Sod off...it was you threw it. (*Pause.*) Fetch it
yourself.

> (*HARRY lifts his hand as if to hit her. She cowers back then
> stands.*)

BELLA: I'll get the bloody ball.

> (*TIM holds her.*)

HARRY: FETCH IT!

> (*MARIE doesn't move. HARRY tries to push her towards the
> woods. She sits suddenly so that he falls across her. She laughs,
> throwing her head back and howling.*
> *HARRY straddles her.*
> *He scoops up a handful of sand and pours some into her
> mouth. She gags, splutters, struggles, but HARRY holds her
> down. He pours sand over her face.*)

BELLA: You BASTARD!

> (*BELLA jumps forward, is held back by TIM.*)

TIM: Shut your mouth.

BELLA: Sod off!

TIM: You want the same? Shut your mouth.

> (*MARIE lies with her mouth and eyes tight closed as HARRY
> pours the sand on to her face. She struggles to avoid it but is
> tightly held.*
> *HARRY empties his hand, scoops up another handful, holds it
> poised above her face.*
> *Pause.*)

HARRY: You gonna fetch the ball now?

> (*MARIE opens her eyes, blinking painfully, stares at HARRY. She spits in his mouth. He falls to the side and she kicks him between the legs and scrambles away.*
>
> *HARRY lies on his knees, propping himself up with one hand, spitting violently into the sand and retching and rubbing his mouth with his free hand, in agony.*
>
> *MARIE sits.*
>
> *TIM steps forward, then stops.*
>
> *BELLA breaks free, goes off, comes back in a second with the ball. She tosses it toward HARRY.*)

BELLA: There's your ball.

> (*BELLA sits down by MARIE, whispers with her. HARRY is still clearing his throat and spitting. When he stops he sits and looks at TIM. TIM stands separate from the others. Pause.*
>
> *TIM walks forward, picks up the ball and throws it hard at MARIE from close range. It hits her on the head and she yelps.*)

TIM: Gonna play?

MARIE: Bugger off!

> (*MARIE's eyes are wet from the stinging pain of the sand, and now the ball. She throws the ball away, wildly.*
>
> *TIM collects it, gives it to HARRY.*
>
> *HARRY holds it for a second, looks at TIM, takes careful aim at MARIE and hits her hard with it on the body.*
>
> *MARIE scrambles away.*
>
> *BELLA tries to intercept the ball but TIM picks it up, takes aim at MARIE.*
>
> *MARIE runs to the right, is barred by HARRY. TIM hits her hard with it on the back. She falls down.*
>
> *BELLA collects the ball. HARRY forces it from her. HARRY hits MARIE on the head with the ball. She sprawls over, scrambles up, hops towards the left, is barred by TIM. He feints to hit her with the ball, she shrinks back. BELLA jumps in front of him.*)

TIM: You want it?

> (*BELLA stands her ground.*

TIM hits her in the face with the ball. She cries, claps her hand to her face, sits.)

BELLA: *(Moans.)* Stop it…stop it! *(Pause.)*

(The ball has rolled centre stage, between HARRY and MARIE. HARRY steps toward it. MARIE steps back, hands up protecting herself.

HARRY stops, looks at MARIE. She looks back at him.

Pause.)

For Christ's sake…stop it!

(HARRY sits down.

Pause.

MARIE sits, wipes her face with the towel. BELLA sits near her, wipes her face. Their movements are very slow. TIM stands looking at the others.

BELLA opens her handbag, offers MARIE some face cream. MARIE takes it, opens it, dabs some on her face. TIM steps forward and grabs the cream.)

TIM: Throw that muck away.

(He looks at the cream in his hand, disgustedly, and hurls it across the dunes.)

MARIE: What's the…

BELLA: He's crazy.

TIM: MUCK! MUCK! MUCK!

(TIM seizes the open handbag. Looks in it with fascinated revulsion. MARIE reaches for it, half-heartedly. TIM ignores her.)

BELLA: Gimme me bag.

TIM: What do you want? *(Roots in the bag.)*

BELLA: Bastard! Gimme the bag.

(TIM begins picking out various items of make-up, holds them at finger-tip, looks at them, tosses them to the sand. BELLA scrambles around trying to recover them, swearing at TIM, sobbing, but no longer attempting to get the bag itself. HARRY watches.)

TIM: What do you want? Mascara? Muck! *(Throws it away.)* Nail varnish? *(Now with increasing intensity.)* Muck! What's this? Perfume? *(Takes out a small bottle, examines it, opens it. Sniffs. Looks sickened.)* 'Passionate

Temptations'...MUCK! (*Drains the bottle in the sand.*)
These...what are these? Eyelashes? False eyelashes!
(*Almost pleading.*) Do you...do you wear these? (*Intense.*)
They're weird. Are they false? Or real? From some poor
bastard coolie's head? Muck! Muck!
(*Throws them away...BELLA scrambles frantically for them.*)

BELLA: ME LASHES! MARIE, ME LASHES!
(*Both girls rake frantically through the sand.*)

TIM: (*Rooting in the bag.*) You carry this filth with you. Filth!
And smear it with your sweat! Muck! (*Takes out a packet
with brush and powder, opens it, smells the brush, looks sick.*)
What's this here? Brush-on powder...'Radiant Beaches!'
(*Bursts out laughing.*) Jesus! RADIANT BEACHES!
(*Throws the powder and the brush into the sand.*)

BELLA: Stop it...for Christ's sake...

TIM: 'Mediterranean Gold'...Suntan? That what this is?
Phoney suntan? That's great. Shit! Shit to smear on your
skin, shit to make you sexy, shit... (*Squeezes some drops
from a tube of sun lotion, looks at his hand, rubs it violently.*)
It's stained me. Shit! Muck! (*Hurls the tube away.*)
(*BELLA scrambles after the tube.*)

BELLA: You swine, you swine!

TIM: This bag...it's covered in muck! Look at it. Like
you...covered in muck. (*Takes out a lipstick.*) What's this?
Lipstick? No...'Lingering Kisses!' Jesus! Lingering
arseholes! Muck, more muck!
(*BELLA snatches at the lipstick. TIM catches her hand.*)
You want this?
(*He daubs a cross on her forehead. She wriggles away, he
holds the bag upside down and empties the contents into the
sand and tosses the bag aside.*)

BELLA: (*Rubbing her forehead.*) You bastard...I'll get you...

MARIE: He's mad.

BELLA: Get the things...
(*The girls scramble around collecting the bits of make-up and
stuffing them in the bag. TIM stands watching. HARRY sits.*)
Let's get out...

MARIE: Sod them...

BELLA: We'll get a lift.

(*MARIE reaches for her stockings, sits to put them on. BELLA reaches for hers. TIM steps forward, picks them up. Pushes BELLA back.*)

Gimme them.

(*TIM holds the stockings dangling.*)

TIM: Do these burn?

BELLA: Gimme me stockings, you bastard!

TIM: (*To HARRY.*) Matches.

(*HARRY gives him a lighter.*
TIM waves the lighter near the foot of the stocking. BELLA makes a grab. HARRY pushes her back.)

(*Threatening with the lighter.*) I'll burn you. Burn you, too.

BELLA: Don't burn them...please.

TIM: You reek.

BELLA: Please don't burn them.

TIM: You reek of piss...and powder.

MARIE: Let's go...never mind them. (*HARRY stops her.*)

(*TIM stands holding the stocking, with the lighter lit, waving it. He speaks in alternating tones of horror and derision, sometimes laughing absurdly at his story.*)

TIM: That smell...is familiar. (*Laughs.*) Years ago I painted a ladies' lavatory. Yeah...a lavo in a club in Slater Street. That was a job I didn't forget...

You musta known the place...in Slater Street. They had a downstairs lavo for the men and an upstairs for the birds...only the birds could go up the stairs. Remember? You remember, Harry?

HARRY: I remember.

TIM: I don't remember the name...anyway, that was the place. I went up there...one Sunday...went up the stairs to paint the lavo. As I was going up the stairs I began to...began to smell it. This sickening smell...I got up the stairs, went through into this lirtle room on the left. There was a dirty little washbowl...no water, I tried it...and this bloody great mirror on the wall. And the place stunk...

I tried to force the window, it wouldn't open. The
lavatory was in the corner. The door was open, you
couldn't lock it. I went in there. Jesus! It stunk of cunt
and...scent. And the strongest was the scent! It smelt...
sweet...made me dizzy... I sat down...yeah... (*Laughing.*)
I had to sit down on the po! It was dark in there...
I thought I was gonna be sick.
There were holes in the door and in the walls. Little
holes drilled through the wood...maybe picked with nail
files...little spy holes...for the birds piping...
And there was this thing on the floor...a rag someone
had left there...a jamrag...left it on the floor of the
lavatory!
So...so I sat there for a while...with that stench...I tried
to breathe through my nose. And I thought of the birds
all collecting up there from the dance downstairs,
standing in front of that bloody great mirror, covering
themselves with muck...and the dust in the washbasin...
an us...us blokes waiting downstairs for the little angels!
In the end I went and stood in front of the mirror, I
looked at meself in the mirror...I started laughing. Yeah.
I laughed. I wanted to go out and stop all the men in the
street and tell them what I had just seen...maybe bring
them back up, give them a look at it...I thought what
they'd say...I was crying with laughter...bloody
hilarious, I couldn't stop.
Then I felt different. Then it didn't...matter, didn't affect
me any more. I opened the door of the lavo, got me
things out...
The walls of the lavo were covered in...words. You
know...just like ours...just the same... 'LICK ME OUT,
BABY'. 'MY BROTHER FEELS ME...' 'MEET ME
HERE AT...'
(*TIM falters. Looks at the stocking. Re-lights the lighter.*)
There was no water in the cistern either. The po was all
bunged up...up near the top: They just kept using it.
BELLA: Gimme that...
TIM: I covered it all in bright orange paint.
(*Pause.*)

BELLA: Gimme that stocking.

TIM: You reek. (*With loathing.*) You stink of sweat...and scent. You oughta be scrubbed with wire wool. You oughta be scraped-down. If I had a blow-lamp now! (*TIM burns the stocking. Nobody else moves.*)

BELLA: (*Sobbing.*) Bastard!

(*TIM burns the other stocking.*)

MARIE: Let's get back...

(*MARIE picks up her bag. TIM seizes it, throws it to HARRY. HARRY holds it. BELLA lunges for it.*)

BELLA: Oh, not that too!

TIM: (*Seizing her.*) You reek. (*Tears at her skirt.*)

BELLA: (*Screaming.*) Leggo of me. Bastard.

TIM: I'm gonna scrub the muck off you. (*TIM forces her toward the beach.*)

HARRY: (*To MARIE.*) You too.

MARIE: Please...

(*MARIE makes a run. HARRY jumps after her. They struggle. He pulls her up and forces her towards the beach.*)

Curtain.

ACT THREE

Now about six o'clock, the light fading a little. HARRY is on his knees, searching through the sand. After a minute, BELLA enters from left. She is wrapped in a blanket.

HARRY: Hi!

BELLA: Hi!

    (*BELLA sits. She watches HARRY searching.*)

HARRY: They've vanished.

BELLA: Hey?

HARRY: The lashes…they've vanished.

    (*Pause. BELLA watches HARRY combing the sand.*)

    I'm probably burying them.

BELLA: You'll never find a pair of lashes in the sand.

HARRY: Don't be too sure…

    (*Pause. HARRY carries on searching.*)

BELLA: They don't matter…

HARRY: Don't they?

BELLA: It's not worth the bother…

HARRY: Listen… Once, we were driving back from here. And one of the girls lost a contact lens. I mean…she dropped it in the car…

BELLA: (*Laughing.*) She dropped it?

HARRY: Well…she lost it in the car.

BELLA: Front or back?

HARRY: Eh?

BELLA: Front or back?

HARRY: Front or back…well…

BELLA: Were you driving?

HARRY: Yeah…anyway…she dropped these lenses…I mean, she dropped a lenses…a lens…

BELLA: How?

HARRY: She was sitting in the back. All I know is, she suddenly screamed out, I've lost me lens!

BELLA: The way you tell a story!

HARRY: So I climbed into the back…and… (*Now lamely.*) …anyway I found her lens.

58

BELLA: Sorry...

HARRY: What?

BELLA: Did I spoil your story?

HARRY: No...no.

　　(*HARRY carries on searching.*

　　BELLA lies back.

　　HARRY picks something up from the sand, and examines it.)

　　Hey!

BELLA: What?

HARRY: What's this?

　　(*BELLA takes it from him.*)

BELLA: (*Laughing.*) A brush.

HARRY: I know it's a brush...what is it?

BELLA: For brushing shades on...

HARRY: Yours?

BELLA: Yeah.

HARRY: Oh...great!

BELLA: All I need now is the stuff to brush on.

HARRY: Christ! Did you lose that too?

BELLA: Yeah...it doesn't matter...

HARRY: (*Cautiously.*) D'you use that stuff?

BELLA: Yeah.

HARRY: You don't need it.

BELLA: I can't get a tan.

HARRY: (*Laughing.*) You don't need a tan.

BELLA: You prefer me pink and horrible?

HARRY: You look great without a tan...you're fair...

BELLA: So are you.

HARRY: That's different.

BELLA: Is it?

HARRY: You don't need a tan.

BELLA: (*Laughing.*) Just as well!

　　(*HARRY carries on searching. He comes up with a tomato.*)

HARRY: Hey!

BELLA: What?

HARRY: Look at this!

BELLA: Food!

HARRY: Liquor!

(*Pause.*

HARRY rolls the tomato down his arm, bounces it on his muscle and catches it.)

Want it?

BELLA: D'you?

HARRY: (*Noble tone.*) We'll save them a bit.

BELLA: Better wait.

HARRY: Yeah…save it till they come back.

(*Both laugh. HARRY sprawls near BELLA.*)

Looks like my eyelash detector has failed.

BELLA: Never mind.

HARRY: They cost much?

BELLA: A few bob. (*Pause.*)

HARRY: You mad?

BELLA: (*Smiles.*) No.

HARRY: Tim's all right.

BELLA: Yeah…

HARRY: Funny.

BELLA: He's all right.

HARRY: I don't know what happened.

BELLA: Doesn't matter. (*Pause.*)

HARRY: He's a good mate.

BELLA: Is he?

HARRY: One of the best. (*Pause.*) The best.

BELLA: Have you known him long?

HARRY: Oh aye, I knew him when he used hair oil.

BELLA: You see a lot of each other?

HARRY: Yeah.

(*Pause.*)

BELLA: Do you…

HARRY: What?

BELLA: The two of you…do you always come here…

HARRY: If we pick anything…

BELLA: If you pick anything up on Saturday night!

HARRY: Usually.

BELLA: Do you always 'end up in the woods'?

HARRY: Not always…

BELLA: But usually…

HARRY: (*Prissy.*) Only if we're pressed...

BELLA: You do that too well.

HARRY: Eh?

BELLA: You could easily be taken for a queer.

HARRY: (*Slightly embarrassed.*) Well...you know better.

BELLA: You could be mistaken for one.

HARRY: It's a way of talking. (*Pause.*)

BELLA: I didn't mean anything.

HARRY: I know.

> (*HARRY plays with BELLA's hair, now falling straight to her shoulders.*)

You look like a mermaid.

BELLA: A mermaid who can't swim.

HARRY: I'll teach you...

BELLA: (*Laughing, but with an edge.*) No thanks...I've had my dip for today. (*Pause.*) Do you usually have sex?

HARRY: (*Mock shock.*) I beg your pardon.

BELLA: When you come out here...

HARRY: It all depends.

BELLA: On the girls?

HARRY: It depends how it works out.

BELLA: How do you mean?

HARRY: Well...one day we came here with a couple of girls. We had a great time. But there was nothing. On the way back we stopped at a pub...I'll never forget this bloke singing *The Wayward Wind*...he was absolutely legless...and whenever any of us looked at each other we were all in fits laughing. It was a great night...and there was nothing. On the way back we stopped the car and climbed over a fence into a field –

BELLA: Oh aye?

HARRY: – no, we were all dying for, you know, and the girls went off down the field in the dark, and when they came back somebody said 'Look at the sky!' because it was all crammed with stars...and we all stood there for a minute like a gang of kids, staring at the stars...and then...we climbed back over the fence and got in the car and drove back and dropped the girls at their place and...that was all... There was nothing.

BELLA: Didn't you fancy them?

HARRY: Don't you believe me?

BELLA: Yeah but –

HARRY: – it sounds funny?

BELLA: Yeah.

HARRY: (*Wry.*) It sounds funny to me too. (*Pause.*)

BELLA: Did you fancy us?

HARRY: Yeah.

BELLA: Did you?

HARRY: (*Laughing.*) You knew that!

BELLA: Yeah…

HARRY: You know that…don't you…
    (*Pause. BELLA idly traces in the sand.*)

BELLA: You courting?

HARRY: Courting?

BELLA: Yeah…going steady…

HARRY: On and off. (*Pause.*) You know…it's nothing
    serious, purely sexual.

BELLA: Is it?

HARRY: Always is.

BELLA: How about your mate?

HARRY: He's crazy about the Reds, wouldn't miss a game.
    (*Pause.*)

BELLA: Did you go to that club?

HARRY: Which?

BELLA: The one he was talking about…the one where he
    was painting…

HARRY: I went in there…couple of times.

BELLA: Did you like it?

HARRY: I didn't rave about it.

BELLA: I used to go there.

HARRY: Did you?

BELLA: Yeah…

HARRY: With your mate?

BELLA: No…a few years back…before I met her.

HARRY: You go with a gang?

BELLA: (*Smiling.*) Yeah…there was a big gang of us.
    (*Laughing.*) We were all crazy.

HARRY: How old?

BELLA: Eh?

HARRY: How old was the gang?

BELLA: Oh, we were all still at school...we had a terrific time. You know...we didn't care about anything...

HARRY: Yeah.

BELLA: Seems ages and ages ago.

HARRY: How old are you now?

BELLA: (*Traces in the sand.*) There.

HARRY: What?

BELLA: There...see?

HARRY: (*Scrutinizing.*) Sixty-nine.

BELLA: That's what I feel!

HARRY: I can't read it...

BELLA: (*Spelling out.*) Over...the...hill

HARRY: You...over the hill?

BELLA: Yeah.

(*Pause. HARRY looks at BELLA, curiously.*)

HARRY: How old are you?

BELLA: Guess.

HARRY: No... I want to know.

BELLA: Why?

HARRY: Nosey.

BELLA: (*Laughs.*) No secret. Nineteen.

HARRY: Nineteen?

BELLA: Yeah.

HARRY: And over the hill?

BELLA: Yeah... (*Pause.*)

HARRY: (*Hot gospelling.*) But look here, young lady! Don't yuh know the whole of life lies ahead of yuh? Think of all the wonderful things life has to offer yuh! Be grateful for the wonderful gifts...

BELLA: The night I was seventeen I cried my eyes out.

HARRY: (*Mildly.*) Did you? (*Pause.*) Why?

(*BELLA shrugs.*)

BELLA: Your mate was right about that club.

HARRY: What? The Ladies?

BELLA: Yeah...

HARRY: Would you feel any better if I told you about the Gents?

BELLA: (*Laughs.*) No thanks! (*Pause.*) Were they just as bad?

HARRY: Worse. (*Pause.*) It's getting cooler isn't it?

BELLA: It's nice.

HARRY: Yeah…

> (*Pause. HARRY looks towards the woods.*)
> They're taking their time…

BELLA: (*Shy giggle.*) Well…

HARRY: (*Prissy.*) Not that I care.

BELLA: There you go…

> (*Pause. They look at each other, look away. BELLA sighs.*)
> Work tomorrow.

HARRY: (*Mock-indignant.*) Don't you like your work?

BELLA: (*Wry.*) Oh yeah!

HARRY: Well…I mean…you'll never make a professional footballer.

BELLA: (*Laughs.*) Noooo…

> (*Pause. HARRY takes out the cigarettes.*)

HARRY: Wanna smoke?

BELLA: Me throat's too dry.

HARRY: We'll get a drink soon.

> (*HARRY takes out a cigarette.*)

BELLA: Here y'are.

> (*She lights it for him. Silence. TIM returns, sits.*)
> Where's Marie?

TIM: (*Smiles.*) Chasing squirrels.

BELLA: (*Amazed.*) Squirrels?

TIM: Yeah. (*Then to HARRY.*) Give us a drag.

> (*HARRY passes the cigarette. TIM puffs it and gives it back.*)
> Ta. I was dying for that.
> (*Pause. TIM looks at the other two.*
> *MARIE returns. Stands.*)

MARIE: (*Excited.*) Hey, Bella…guess what we saw in the woods.

BELLA: A squirrel.

MARIE: (*Disappointed.*) Oh. (*Then to TIM.*) You told them.

BELLA: What was it like?

MARIE: (*Eager.*) It was red. A red squirrel…in the woods.

HARRY: (*Grins.*) Have you never seen a squirrel before?

MARIE: (*Straight.*) No.

BELLA: Neither have I.

TIM: It came right up to us.

MARIE: Yeah! It wasn't frightened or anything.

HARRY: You can feed them.

MARIE: (*Thrilled.*) Feed them? Can you?

HARRY: Yeah...there's a Squirrel Reserve...further up the beach...and the squirrels come right up to the wire netting and stick their heads through for food.

MARIE: Go way!

HARRY: They do. Don't they, Tim?

TIM: Yeah. They're not shy. You can feed them.

MARIE: Isn't that great!

BELLA: I'd love to do that.

MARIE: Yeah...I would too.

BELLA: Could we do that?

HARRY: What are we gonna feed them?

MARIE: (*Wry.*) Oh aye. (*They chuckle.*)

BELLA: I'd love that, though. I'd love to feed them.

TIM: Do it another time.

MARIE: What do you feed them?

HARRY: Smoky bacon crisps.

MARIE: You what?

HARRY: Smoky bacon crisps.

MARIE: (*Laughs.*) Crisp off!

HARRY: (*Injured.*) You do.

MARIE: (*Hooting.*) Smoky bacon crisps!

HARRY: They'll touch nothing else.

MARIE: I thought they ate nuts?

HARRY: Noooo...smoky bacon crisps or nothing. That's their diet. (*Pause.*) If you catch one young it makes a very tasty dinner.

MARIE: Oh...sod off!

HARRY: Smoky bacon squirrel...delicious.

MARIE: Ughhh.

(*The foursome sit in a circle. Pause.*)

(*To BELLA.*) You haven't half caught the sun!

BELLA: Yeah...I'm burning.

MARIE: Have I?

BELLA: You're all red.

MARIE: Great! (*Sly grin.*) I'm sore too...

BELLA: (*Chuckles.*) Oohhh...was he rough?

MARIE: Wild.

TIM: I was driven to it.

> (*Silence. BELLA goes to the top of the dune, looks across the river. She hitches the towel across her shoulders and comes down.*)

MARIE: You look like the Queen of the May.

BELLA: (*Smiles.*) I was the Queen of the May!

MARIE: Oh aye?

BELLA: Two years running. I was made up with meself. Two years running I was picked to lead the procession down our street. I had long blonde hair...real blonde... and I had me ma's dress on, and me sister's shoes, and lace curtains for a veil, and I went clumping along at the head of the procession, two years running. I thought I was lovely. (*Pause. Laughs, wry.*) Then I got me National Health specs and nobody wanted to know. Huh...I wouldn't go out in them, anyway. (*Pause.*) Still...I was the Queen of the May...two years running...I've got a photograph of...I looked lovely...with me long blonde hair...looked a little angel!

> (*Silence.*)

HARRY: (*To TIM.*) Were you ever the Queen of the May?

TIM: I was invited. They were very keen.

HARRY: Too shy, were you?

TIM: I never liked processions. (*Pause.*)

> (*MARIE roots in the bag.*)

MARIE: I'm starving.

> (*HARRY picks up a half-eaten sandwich, offers it.*)

HARRY: Here y'are.

> (*MARIE takes it, examines it delicately, bites it.*)

MARIE: (*Crunching.*) It's all fulla sand.

> (*MARIE slings it aside. Silence. She looks at HARRY.*)
>
> (*Sly grin.*) Was your mam up early this morning?

HARRY: Me mam?

MARIE: Yeah.

HARRY: What about me mam?

MARIE: Was she up early this morning?

HARRY: Me mam's always up early.

MARIE: She musta been up early this morning.

HARRY: Eh?

(*Pause. MARIE looks at BELLA.*)

MARIE: (*Grins.*) Who made the butties?

HARRY: You what?

MARIE: Who made the butties?

(*Silence. HARRY glances at TIM.*)

Who made the butties then?

HARRY: Me.

MARIE: Very nice.

HARRY: (*Ultra polite.*) I'm glad you liked them.

MARIE: Oh, they were very nice.

(*HARRY stares at her. MARIE grins back, glances at BELLA, giggles. HARRY looks, glances at TIM, lies back. Silence.*)

HARRY: (*Sits up.*) I'm so glad you approve.

(*HARRY lies back. MARIE giggles. She looks around, licks her lips.*)

MARIE: I'm dying of thirst.

BELLA: Hey...wanna tomato?

MARIE: What?

(*BELLA offers the tomato.*)

BELLA: D'you want it?

MARIE: I'll wait for a drink.

TIM: Pubs'll be open soon.

BELLA: (*To TIM.*) D'you want it?

HARRY: (*Noble.*) We saved that for you.

TIM: Gee...shucks!

(*TIM bites the tomato, passes it to BELLA.*)

BELLA: Ta...

(*BELLA sucks the tomato, tosses the remains into the sand – PLOP! Silence. The men lie back.*)

MARIE: (*Pokes HARRY.*) Where did you get the gloves?

HARRY: You what?

MARIE: Where did you get the gloves?

HARRY: What gloves?

MARIE: The gloves in the van.

HARRY: In the van?

MARIE: I seen a pair of gloves in the van.

HARRY: Did you?

MARIE: (*Arch.*) Ladies' gloves.

HARRY: What sharp eyes we have!

MARIE: They were in the glove compartment.

HARRY: I keep all my gloves there.

MARIE: Oh aye?

HARRY: Yeah.

MARIE: Whose is they?

HARRY: Me mam's.

MARIE: (*Sarcastic.*) Oh aye!

HARRY: I gave her a lift to the Post Office.

MARIE: Did you?

HARRY: She won't go out without her gloves on.

MARIE: Won't she?

HARRY: She leaves gloves all over the place.

MARIE: Does she?

HARRY: I'm forever clearing up after her. (*Pause.*)

BELLA: (*To HARRY, smiling.*) Are you courting?

TIM: (*Flicks his wrist.*) No, we're just good friends.

    (*BELLA laughs. HARRY lies back. Silence. MARIE looks up.*)

MARIE: Got any ciggies?

HARRY: One.

    (*HARRY passes the cigarette, gives her a light.*)

MARIE: (*To BELLA.*) Wanna drag?

BELLA: Ta. (*BELLA puffs, offers it to HARRY.*) D'you wanna drag?

HARRY: Ta. (*HARRY puffs, offers it to TIM.*)

TIM: Ta. (*TIM puffs, offers it back to MARIE.*)

MARIE: I'm too dry.

BELLA: Yeah…I'm parched.

HARRY: They'll soon be open.

TIM: What time is it?

    (*HARRY gets up and elaborately studies the sun.*)

HARRY: Twenty-eight – no! Twenty-nine minutes past six. (*Sits.*) I could just go a pint of bitter. (*Pause.*)

TIM: (*Licking his lips.*) Yeah…

    (*Silence. HARRY snaps on the radio, tahes BELLA's hand, stands.*)

HARRY: Let's have a dance.

BELLA: (*Delighted.*) Yeah.

(*They dance.*)

TIM: (*Ultra polite, to MARIE.*) May I have this dance, please?

MARIE: (*Disdainful.*) Yeah...all right...

(*They dance.*

After a moment, quite naturally, HARRY is facing MARIE and dancing with her. After this the couples dissolve and the foursome dance together. Then HARRY faces MARIE again and begins to clown.)

HARRY: Come on...

MARIE: (*Laughing.*) Jesus!

HARRY: (*Mock indignant.*) Come on...you're not doing it properly.

MARIE: Where did you learn to dance?

HARRY: All my steps are my own, darling.

(*MARIE tries to copy him, but falls back laughing. TIM taps him on the shoulder.*)

TIM: May I cut in?

HARRY: (*Queer tone.*) Certainly.

(*The men dance – ballroom style. The girls look at them, laughing. Then the girls dance, half-heartedly.*)

TIM: Have you been unfaithful again?

HARRY: (*Hanging his head.*) Yes.

TIM: Swine.

HARRY: Sorry... (*Pause.*) Have you?

TIM: Yes.

HARRY: With them?

TIM: Yeah...

HARRY: Swine.

MARIE: Cheeky buggers!

(*MARIE snaps off the transistor. The four sit down.*)

(*To HARRY – sly grin.*) You know last night...

HARRY: What?

MARIE: What made you pick us?

HARRY: Pick you?

MARIE: Yeah...why did you pick us?

(*Pause. HARRY grins.*)

HARRY: You were sitting next to us.

MARIE: Oh, thanks very much!

HARRY: Pleasure.

MARIE: You came and sat next to us. You were sitting
    somewhere else when we came in. I saw you.

HARRY: Oh aye...piping?

MARIE: Huh!

HARRY: No...what it was...I fancied the barmaid, see.

MARIE: Oh aye? The Chinese girl?

HARRY: She's only part time.

MARIE: Oh?

HARRY: Well, I was chatting her up, like, and –

MARIE: She didn't fancy you?

HARRY: She was crazy about me. She kept sending me
    drinks over.

MARIE: What went wrong?

TIM: She didn't have a mate.

HARRY: So we looked around...and we decided you'd do...

MARIE: (*Giggling.*) Cheeky sod! (*Silence.*)

BELLA: (*To HARRY.*) Hey...can we go to that pub...

HARRY: What pub?

BELLA: You know...the one you were talking about...where
    you went that time before...the one where they had the
    sing-song...

HARRY: (*Looks at TIM.*) Could do...

BELLA: I'd love to go somewhere like that. A singing pub.

MARIE: Yeah...

TIM: It's a bit out of the way, that one...

BELLA: In the country...?

TIM: Yeah...

BELLA: It sounds nice...

HARRY: Fancy going back to Liverpool?

TIM: Plenty of pubs there.

MARIE: I'm fed up drinking in town.

BELLA: Let's go to a country pub...eh?

    (*Pause.*)

TIM: We'll have a look on the way back.

(*HARRY stands, puts on his sweater, climbs the dune and looks across the river.*)

HARRY: Hey…look at this!

BELLA: (*Joining him.*) What is it?

HARRY: A liner…on its way to South America.

BELLA: (*Laughing.*) How do you know it's going to South America?

HARRY: (*Pompous.*) All liners go to South America!

BELLA: Wish we were on it.

HARRY: (*Stares at her.*) Have you ever thought of joining the Fire Service?

BELLA: Oh sure!

(*Pause. They watch the liner.*)

HARRY: When I was a kid I used to lie awake and listen to the foghorns from the river…the sounds of the ships… the liners going… (*Deep-voiced.*) BEEEEMMMMMM and the little tugs piping… (*Shrill.*) YIPYIPYIP…and the others going…WHOOWHOOWHOO.

BELLA: I'd be a little tug! YIPYIPYIP.

HARRY: BEEEMMMMM.

BELLA: WHOOWHOOWHOO.

HARRY: BEEEEMMMMMM.

BELLA: YIPYIPYIP.

HARRY: BEEEMMMMM.

(*TIM comes behind them.*)

TIM: WHOOWHOOWHOO.

BELLA: YIPYIPYIP.

MARIE: YIPYIPYIP.

(*MARIE stands and joins them. They clown around.*)

HARRY: BEEEEMMMMMMMM.

TIM: WHOOWHOOWHOO.

MARIE: YIPYIPYIP.

BELLA: YIPYIPYIP.

TIM: BEEEEMMMMMM.

(*HARRY suddenly comes down and sits sulking.*)

HARRY: Not playing any more.

TIM: (*Joins him.*) What's the matter?

HARRY: (*Petulant.*) Not talking.

TIM: (*Grins.*) Oh…I'm sorry.

HARRY: (*Outburst.*) I was the liner.

TIM: Were you?

HARRY: You would have to be a liner as well.

TIM: (*Laughing.*) I'll be a canoe if you like…

HARRY: Not speaking.

(*Pause.*)

BELLA: (*Wry.*) Work tomorrow.

MARIE: Yeah…

(*Pause.*)

BELLA: Let's have a great night out.

MARIE: (*Eager.*) Yeah.

BELLA: Yeah.

TIM: What time is it?

HARRY: Nearly seven.

TIM: Jesus! We'll soon be in drinking time.

MARIE: Well come 'ead then!

BELLA: Yeah.

(*They start to dress.*

TIM is putting on his shoes when he stops and stares. Takes something out.)

TIM: Hey!

MARIE: What?

TIM: Look at this!

BELLA: The lashes! Great!

HARRY: And I searched the bloody sandhill.

BELLA: Great! Now I can go out in style!

(*MARIE helps BELLA put the lashes on. The men sit waiting and watching.*)

How's that?

HARRY: Let's see you blink.

(*BELLA blinks and puts on a vamp expression.*)

I'll have to get a pair of those meself!

(*The girls make up.*

This is a long session, uninterrupted except for the occasional giggle from the girls, with the men sitting watching motionless, and the transistor playing. The session is prolonged to the point of acute impatience.

72

Each girl applies face cream...eye shadow...eye liner...
mascara...eyebrow pencil...lipstick...)

MARIE: (*To TIM.*) Wanna try some? (*Laughing.*)

TIM: (*Mock vanity.*) Oh... I rely on my bone structure.

(*When the facial treatment is completed, MARIE holds up*
the mirror while BELLA back-combs her hair and then sprays
it with lacquer; BELLA then holds the mirror while MARIE
does her hair. Each girl then applies perfume to her neck,
ears, chest and wrists. As appropriate, the girls apply the
perfume to each other. The girls collect their things together.)

MARIE: You right?

BELLA: Yeah...

MARIE: Before we go... (*Nods towards the woods.*)

BELLA: Oh yeah...

MARIE: (*To TIM.*) Just a quick one. (*Laughs.*)

(*The men begin to collect the orange peel, papers etc., and put*
them in a newspaper. They stop and look at each other. TIM
holds up a towel.)

TIM: Smell that.

HARRY: (*Rolling his eyes.*) Phew...

TIM: There's orange peel all over the place...

(*TIM throws down some peelings. The two men look at each*
other and grin.)

HARRY: You're thinking what I'm thinking.

(*BELLA comes on, followed by MARIE. MARIE stops at the*
top of the dune. She holds her skirt high and rubs her leg.)

MARIE: (*Laughing.*) Sorry, lads...it's the drips!

(*The men stare.*)

You right?

TIM: Yeah...go on...we'll just finish getting the things.

(*The girls go off right.*
The men stand still, looking at each other for a minute. TIM
grins. HARRY closes his eyes and laughs quietly.)

HARRY: It's the drips!

TIM: We better hurry up.

(*They finish collecting their things hastily.*)

HARRY: If we cut through the woods we'll get to the van
well before them.

TIM: We don't wanna take any chances.

HARRY: No…

TIM: We better move.

HARRY: Yeah…they'll get a lift.

TIM: (*Laughs.*) They'll get a lift!

HARRY: Let's get out.

TIM: We'll just make it for Benediction!

HARRY: I'm dying for a pint…

TIM: Where'll we go?

HARRY: The opposite way from here.

(*TIM kicks sand over the pile of peelings, etc.*)

TIM: Go quiet while we're in the wood…

HARRY: …then we can run…

TIM: …run like buggery!

(*HARRY picks up the transistor and turns it off. They exit left to the woods.*)

HARRY: (*Laughing.*) Dirty cows!

TIM: (*Laughing.*) Dirty cows!

Curtain.

ALPHA BETA

for Kathleen and Kate and Helen

Characters

MR ELLIOT

MRS ELLIOT

The action of the play occurs in the lounge of the
Elliots' home in Liverpool, over a period of nine
years. When the play opens Mr Elliot is twenty-nine
and Mrs Elliot twenty-six.

ACT ONE: 1000 Women – Winter 1962
ACT TWO: Pseudomorph 1966
ACT THREE: Alpha Beta – Summer, 1971

Alpha Beta opened at the Royal Court Theatre on 26 January 1972 and subsequently transferred to the Apollo Theatre, with the following cast:

MR ELLIOT, Albert Finney

MRS ELLIOT, Rachel Roberts

Director Anthony Page

Designer Alan Tagg

The play was presented by the Royal Court Theatre and Memorial Enterprises.

Production Note

Alpha Beta is partly a study of moral conditioning but also explores the problem of a relationship in which, for complex reasons, one party is immeasurably more committed than the other. In production, these levels can be suggested by maintaining a minute naturalism on the surface but allowing certain actions (e.g. the wallpapering) and objects (e.g. the bicycle) to attain a significance beyond their immediate context.

It is also important to suggest the areas of ambiguity in the two characters: in the woman, between 'Norma Elliot', the vulnerable and passionate human being, and 'Mrs Elliot', the implacable wife, completely committed to the standards brainwashed into her; and in the man, between the 'social catalyst' (as he sees himself), and the pub orator and permanent adolescent forever justifying his own sexual capriciousness (as she certainly sees him).

In the Royal Court production there was one interval, between Acts II and III. Photographs of working-class weddings and suburban family life were flashed on to a screen between Acts I and II. Each Act was preceded by popular music appropriate to the period of the Act.

Ted Whitehead

ACT ONE
1000 Women

Winter, 1962. The time is about 11:15 p.m. A lounge. MRS ELLIOT is decorating. She wears a scarf round her head and a pair of overalls.

She is putting new white wallpaper over the old faded orange and has nearly finished the room. She has already painted the ceiling and the woodwork white.

Decorating materials and equipment are spread across the floor, which has been protected with newspapers, and the furniture is all stacked to one side. She hears MR ELLIOT and hurries.

MR ELLIOT comes in. He is dressed smartly but in a very conservative style-belted raincoat, navy blue suit and tie, white shirt, black shoes. He pushes his way in, looks around. Then, in silence, ignoring MRS ELLIOT's glance, he picks his way delicately through the equipment and goes into the kitchen and shuts the door.

MRS ELLIOT looks after him, then resumes her work. She works very competently and seems engrossed in it.

After a moment MR ELLIOT returns with a coffee. He studies the furniture. Parks himself on the corner of a chair, rather awkwardly. MRS ELLIOT turns round to look at him. He ignores her and scrutinizes the room. She smiles, speaks lightly.

MRS ELLIOT: Thank you…I would like a coffee…
MR ELLIOT: What?
MRS ELLIOT: Yes…I would like a coffee.
MR ELLIOT: Do you have to have a coffee just because I'm having a coffee?
MRS ELLIOT: I just *feel* like a coffee…
MR ELLIOT: As soon as *I* have a coffee you just feel like a coffee?
MRS ELLIOT: Yes!
MR ELLIOT: What do you feel like when I have a crap?
(*Silence.*)

MRS ELLIOT: I've been a very good girl today…worked from dawn to dusk.

MR ELLIOT: Dawn to dawn, you mean.

MRS ELLIOT: It'll soon be finished. (*Pause.*) It'll look nice when it's finished.

(*Silence. MR ELLIOT surveys the room.*)

MR ELLIOT: You don't think…

MRS ELLIOT: What?

MR ELLIOT: You don't think it suffers from a certain… monotony?

MRS ELLIOT: Monotony?

MR ELLIOT: All this white?

MRS ELLIOT: Oh…I don't know. No. I think it'll look nice…

MR ELLIOT: When it's finished?

MRS ELLIOT: Yes.

MR ELLIOT: At least it will look newly decorated.

MRS ELLIOT: You must admit it was ready for it.

MR ELLIOT: I wouldn't dispute that.

(*Silence. MRS ELLIOT turns to resume work. She stops when MR ELLIOT speaks.*)

I see you've repaired the fence, too.

MRS ELLIOT: What?

MR ELLIOT: You've repaired the fence in the road.

MRS ELLIOT: Oh…that. Yes. It didn't take long. (*Pause.*) I've only fixed it with wire…

MR ELLIOT: Very enterprising.

MRS ELLIOT: You don't…mind, do you?

MR ELLIOT: Mind?

MRS ELLIOT: About me repairing the fence?

MR ELLIOT: No doubt the neighbours will admire your initiative.

(*Silence.*)

Don't let me interrupt your work.

(*MRS ELLIOT resumes work.*

MR ELLIOT inspects his paperback books, re-stacks them. Then he settles back, sips his coffee. He studies his watch.)

MRS ELLIOT: Why don't you go to bed?

MR ELLIOT: I'm not tired.

MRS ELLIOT: Oh... (*Silence.*)

Have you had anything to eat?

MR ELLIOT: No.

MRS ELLIOT: I'll make a snack...when I've done this bit.

MR ELLIOT: I don't want anything to eat.

MRS ELLIOT: Did you have a drink?

MR ELLIOT: What?

MRS ELLIOT: Did you...have a drink?

MR ELLIOT: Yes!

(*MR ELLIOT sits staring at his watch.*
MRS ELLIOT turns away as if to work. Looks at the wall.)

In half an hour I'll be twenty-nine.

MRS ELLIOT: (*Light.*) We'll open a tin of sardines and celebrate!

MR ELLIOT: (*Moody.*) In twelve months and half an hour I'll be thirty. (*Pause.*) Christ.

(*MRS ELLIOT hastens to finish the wallpapering.*)

MRS ELLIOT: Where did you go?

MR ELLIOT: What?

MRS ELLIOT: Where did you go...for a drink?

MR ELLIOT: The Basnett Bar. (*Pause.*) The others went on to a club.

MRS ELLIOT: Oh...

MR ELLIOT: With Billy.

MRS ELLIOT: Billy?

MR ELLIOT: We met him at the beach once with his wife. Remember? She was a tall dark girl...very attractive.

MRS ELLIOT: Oh...I remember. With a little baby? A baby girl...

MR ELLIOT: That's right.

MRS ELLIOT: I remember.

MR ELLIOT: He buried her a week ago.

MRS ELLIOT: Oh...who?

MR ELLIOT: His wife.

MRS ELLIOT: She was...very young...wasn't she?

MR ELLIOT: You mean young to die?

MRS ELLIOT: Yes.

MR ELLIOT: (*Flip.*) You're never too young to die.

MRS ELLIOT: What happened?

MR ELLIOT: She went into hospital a year ago with a lump on her breast. They cut the lump out. Then after a few months she went back in and they cut the breast off. Then, after a little more time, she went back and they diagnosed cancer of the stomach. Inoperable. She died the week before last.

MRS ELLIOT: Oh...isn't that...horrible...

MR ELLIOT: We haven't seen Billy for a few months now. (*Pause.*) Anyway, he turned up tonight again.

MRS ELLIOT: How was he?

MR ELLIOT: I asked him that very question. I was wondering how he was getting on...how he was managing with the kids, and so on...and when we were on our own for a minute – standing in the bog, actually – I said to him: 'I heard about your wife.' He hadn't spoken about it to us. Anyway, I said I was sorry, and he said: 'Oh...yes.' So then I said: 'How are you getting on?' And he said: 'I feel like a fifteen-year-old! I'm having the time of my fucking life!'

MRS ELLIOT: He's probably still affected by shock...

MR ELLIOT: You *would* say that.

MRS ELLIOT: Well...he may be!

MR ELLIOT: Yeah...the shock of freedom.

(*MRS ELLIOT turns grimly to her work. MR ELLIOT hangs his coat in the hall and takes a paperback from the pocket.*)

MRS ELLIOT: Who else was there?

MR ELLIOT: Oh...Harry, Jim, the usual crowd.

MRS ELLIOT: And did they go on to the club?

MR ELLIOT: Well...some of them.

MRS ELLIOT: Huh... It's pathetic!

MR ELLIOT: Don't start that...

MRS ELLIOT: What?

MR ELLIOT: All that stuff about mutton dressed as ram.

(*He comes back in. Takes some money from a pay packet and slips it into an exercise book.*)

MRS ELLIOT: It *is* pathetic. (*Pause.*) And what...what stopped you?

MR ELLIOT: I don't know. (*Pause.*) I wasn't in the mood.

MRS ELLIOT: The mood for what?

MR ELLIOT: (*Flat.*) Adventure.

(*He throws away the pay packet and puts the remaining money in his pocket.*)

MRS ELLIOT: Huh!

MR ELLIOT: No...my birthday had set me thinking...

MRS ELLIOT: Looking back over the years of waste?

MR ELLIOT: Looking forward over the years of waste.

MRS ELLIOT: That's...up to you...

MR ELLIOT: What's up to me? I'm a man-who's-about-to-be-twenty-nine...and next year I shall be a man-who's-about-to-be-thirty...and after that I shall be a man who's about-to-be-forty. I feel toothless and superseded.
(*Laughs.*) Christ...I feel that if I paid a compliment to a pretty girl she'd assume I *wasn't* making a pass!

MRS ELLIOT: Of course you want to pay compliments to pretty girls.

MR ELLIOT: Of course.

MRS ELLIOT: I think you, and your crowd, are completely pathetic...running round the clubs like a gang of teenagers, when every one of you has a wife...and a family.

MR ELLIOT: The teenagers don't have to run round the clubs. (*Silence. MRS ELLIOT is finishing off the wall.*) We had a very interesting debate tonight.

MRS ELLIOT: Did you?

MR ELLIOT: About the quality of working-class morality. Most of the crowd – who have of course now assumed middle-class status – agreed that working-class morality was loose and depraving: I argued that it was rigid and depraving.

MRS ELLIOT: Depraving?

MR ELLIOT: Yes, because it's a stallion-style morality... The principle is very simple: the male pokes everything he can get until one day he inadvertently pokes himself into wedlock; after that he stops poking and starts lusting. The morality is rigid because, once married, the

83

male never actually pokes anything else; and it's depraved because he lusts his life away in masculine obscenities and dirty jokes.

MRS ELLIOT: WHOOPS!

(*MRS ELLIOT struggles to secure a strip of paper that is peeling from the ceiling. She stands on a ladder to press it back.*

MR ELLIOT sits watching.

She climbs down.)

My arms are aching…

(*She goes out for a coffee.*)

MR ELLIOT: (*Calls.*) Do you agree?

MRS ELLIOT: (*Calls.*) D'you want a coffee?

(*MR ELLIOT lights a cigarette, looking impatient.*)

MR ELLIOT: Do you agree with my views of working-class morality?

(*MRS ELLIOT returns with two coffees. She puts one down by MR ELLIOT, and perches on a chair with the other.*)

MRS ELLIOT: Is that your morality?

MR ELLIOT: Yes. It's a pity I can never remember dirty jokes.

MRS ELLIOT: What did Harry think?

MR ELLIOT: About what?

MRS ELLIOT: Working-class morality…

MR ELLIOT: He thought it was rigid and not depraving.

MRS ELLIOT: Did he go to the club?

MR ELLIOT: No.

MRS ELLIOT: I agree with him.

MR ELLIOT: About what?

MRS ELLIOT: Working-class morality.

(*MR ELLIOT stares at her in exaggerated astonishment.*)

MR ELLIOT: *You* agree with him!

MRS ELLIOT: (*Defensive.*) Yes… I do…

MR ELLIOT: (*Ironic.*) I'm sure your father would be delighted to hear that.

(*Pause.*)

MRS ELLIOT: My father?

MR ELLIOT: Yes.

MRS ELLIOT: I don't see what he has to do with it.

MR ELLIOT: He's a classic example of what I mean about working-class morality.

(*Pause.*)

MRS ELLIOT: How is he?

MR ELLIOT: You're always ranting on about how unfair he is to your mother...gives her a dog's life, you say. (*Pause.*) You said he was the soul of generosity in the alehouse and a monster of meanness at home.

MRS ELLIOT: What's that got to do with...sexual morality? He's never played around...

MR ELLIOT: Precisely! That's why he's a classical example!

MRS ELLIOT: Why?

MR ELLIOT: He only really comes alive in the company of his alehouse cronies. You ought to hear him with them.

MRS ELLIOT: What ought I to hear?

MR ELLIOT: (*Teasing.*) Or perhaps you ought not to hear it.

MRS ELLIOT: Hear what?

MR ELLIOT: His jokes.

MRS ELLIOT: What jokes?

MR ELLIOT: As I said, I have a very poor memory.

MRS ELLIOT: You mean dirty jokes. (*Silence.*) You mean dirty jokes, don't you?

MR ELLIOT: Yes.

MRS ELLIOT: (*Heated.*) I don't believe it.

MR ELLIOT: I laugh, of course.

MRS ELLIOT: I bet you howl.

MR ELLIOT: No...no, I don't howl... (*Judiciously.*) I curl my lips and laugh.

MRS ELLIOT: (*Contemptuously.*) I bet you do.

MR ELLIOT: Actually I feel more like puking.

MRS ELLIOT: I don't believe you...about the jokes.

MR ELLIOT: I'm not...attacking your father.

MRS ELLIOT: HUH!

MR ELLIOT: I mean...they all do it. They all rival each other in the dirtiness of their jokes. Basically, they vent their hatred of women through the jokes. They mock their own dependence on women and feel stronger for it.

The more the jokes degrade women, the more they like it, and the more they laugh. (*Pause.*) Your father's no exception.

MRS ELLIOT: It's sickening.

MR ELLIOT: If the men didn't tell jokes they'd probably beat the women up.

MRS ELLIOT: Sickening…especially when I think of how he treated me.

MR ELLIOT: (*Curious.*) Treated you?

MRS ELLIOT: He was a tyrant. Even when I was in my teens, he insisted on my being back in the house every night by nine o'clock! Nine o'clock…although he was never back in until well after the pubs shut, naturally. (*Pause.*) And when he did come back in…he'd conduct a detailed interrogation as to where I'd been, who with, what I'd done or hadn't done…

MR ELLIOT: He was protecting you from your libidinous teenage impulses.

MRS ELLIOT: He didn't need to.

MR ELLIOT: (*Ironic.*) You…didn't have any libidinous teenage impulses?

MRS ELLIOT: I didn't need any protection.

MR ELLIOT: What? No lustful gallants eager to give you your first experience? Your first tender, never-to-be-forgotten grope?

MRS ELLIOT: (*Contemptuous.*) There's never any shortage of 'lustful gallants'.

MR ELLIOT: (*Pompous.*) I should hope not! (*Silence. Serious tone.*) I suppose, what it was with your old man was that…having got your mother 'into trouble', as they say, over you…he wanted to make sure that he didn't allow the same to happen to you.

MRS ELLIOT: (*Puzzled.*) 'Over me'?

MR ELLIOT: Yes.

(*Silence.*)

MRS ELLIOT: Do you mean what you appear to mean?

MR ELLIOT: Yes.

MRS ELLIOT: You're going too far.

MR ELLIOT: (*Sincere tone.*) He told me.

MRS ELLIOT: (*Cynical.*) He told you what?

MR ELLIOT: He told me that when he got married, he *had* to…because his wife already had a bun in the oven. That bun was you.

MRS ELLIOT: I don't believe you.

MR ELLIOT: Ask him.

MRS ELLIOT: I'll do better than that – I'll ask her.

MR ELLIOT: (*Reflective.*) Though…for myself…I'd certainly prefer to believe that I was conceived in some wild and furtive fuck than in the routine copulations of marriage.

MRS ELLIOT: It's romantic to think so, but you probably were.

MR ELLIOT: (*Smiles.*) I like to think so. (*Pause.*) It's odd, come to think of it, that we *didn't* have the usual pressing reason for wedlock, did we? Why the hell did we get married?

MRS ELLIOT: You wanted to.

MR ELLIOT: Didn't you?

MRS ELLIOT: Yes. No.

MR ELLIOT: What?

MRS ELLIOT: I didn't really want to…

MR ELLIOT: You wanted to escape from your father.

MRS ELLIOT: (*Cynical.*) Escape…to what?

MR ELLIOT: (*Hand on heart.*) ME!

MRS ELLIOT: Huh! Prince Charming!

MR ELLIOT: (*Romantic.*) Yes…there you were, trapped in the ogre's castle…when one day, I came galloping by and swept you off your feet and…and then we got married and lived miserably ever after. That's the new conclusion, that, to the old fairy tale. (*Then bitterly.*) You were desperate to get married…when I met you.

MRS ELLIOT: (*Cool.*) You weren't the only Prince Charming around.

MR ELLIOT: (*Savage.*) If I hadn't married you, you would have ended up a grey-haired virgin!

MRS ELLIOT: That's one thing I regret…

MR ELLIOT: Eh?

MRS ELLIOT: I 'saved' myself.

MR ELLIOT: (*Mock shock.*) I beg your pardon?

MRS ELLIOT: I 'saved' myself. (*Laughs derisively.*) For you!
What a joke!

(*MR ELLIOT glances sourly at her.*)

For a long time, for years in fact...before I met you...I
was courting a man that I was very fond of...but I
wouldn't let him touch me. (*Laughs.*) Huh! I wouldn't let
him anywhere near me.

MR ELLIOT: Your father evidently did a very good job.

MRS ELLIOT: (*Wry, sad.*) Yes...

MR ELLIOT: And so this man that you were fond of...

MRS ELLIOT: Yes.

MR ELLIOT: (*Brutal.*) And so he dumped you?

MRS ELLIOT: (*Level.*) More or less.

MR ELLIOT: THE BOUNDER!

MRS ELLIOT: He was twice the man you are.

MR ELLIOT: Naturally, now he's gone.

MRS ELLIOT: I wasn't ready to marry him...but I could
have given him that.

MR ELLIOT: You make it sound like a Christmas present.

MRS ELLIOT: It was hardly worth 'saving' for you,
anyway, was it?

MR ELLIOT: Me? I didn't ask you to save it.

MRS ELLIOT: (*Laughs.*) You wouldn't marry anyone who
wasn't a virgin. You're one of the very worst cases of the
working-class morality you've been attacking... You
were infected at an early age and I doubt if you'll ever
recover. You're a real pillar of morality.

MR ELLIOT: I'm a pillar of the *new* morality.

MRS ELLIOT: You really are a classic example of the
working-class buck. You don't come in rotten drunk –

MR ELLIOT: – because I can hold my ale.

MRS ELLIOT: – and you don't throw your dinner on the
floor like my father sometimes did –

MR ELLIOT: – because I don't get any dinner.

MRS ELLIOT: You could do!

MR ELLIOT: Oh, no, oh no. We agreed, after a long succession of incinerated dinners, that if I didn't get in before nine o'clock, I should get no dinner. Which suits me fine, since it removes your only excuse for attacking me when — as always — I come home after nine.

MRS ELLIOT: ...you *don't* swear at the children and you don't beat me up...

MR ELLIOT: I'm beginning to feel quite saintly!

MRS ELLIOT: ...But essentially, you're no different from my father. (*Pause.*) Worse, in fact.

MR ELLIOT: (*Mock shock.*) Worse?

MRS ELLIOT: You couldn't call my father unfaithful.

MR ELLIOT: I didn't call your father unfaithful.

MRS ELLIOT: No. (*Silence.*)

MR ELLIOT: You think I am unfaithful?

MRS ELLIOT: Aren't you?

MR ELLIOT: No such luck.

MRS ELLIOT: Huh. (*Pause.*)

MR ELLIOT: I have not been unfaithful.

MRS ELLIOT: For lack of opportunity?

MR ELLIOT: Yes. (*Pause; he reflects.*) Well, to put it more precisely, for lack of courage to create the opportunity or to exploit the opportunity when offered.

MRS ELLIOT: A faithful coward?

MR ELLIOT: Yes.

MRS ELLIOT: What are you afraid of then?

MR ELLIOT: I'm afraid of being thought a dirty old man.

MRS ELLIOT: Which you are...

MR ELLIOT: Only in...my secret wishes. (*Whispers.*) It's our secret! Nobody knows...except you and me! (*MR ELLIOT puts his finger to his lips; picks up a newspaper. MRS ELLIOT busies herself tidying up. She stops.*)

MRS ELLIOT: Would you?

MR ELLIOT: Would I what?

(*Pause. MRS ELLIOT forces herself to speak.*)

MRS ELLIOT: Fuck someone?

(*MR ELLIOT reflects.*)

MR ELLIOT: Present company excluded?

MRS ELLIOT: There's no danger of that!

MR ELLIOT: I wouldn't touch *you* with a bargepole, of course.

MRS ELLIOT: You won't be offered the opportunity.

MR ELLIOT: Fine.

MRS ELLIOT: But you *would* fuck someone else?
  (*Silence. MR ELLIOT reflects. She stares at him.*)

MR ELLIOT: I suppose...speaking hypothetically, of course...it is conceivable that if I were caught in the right mood...if, for instance, I were relaxing at a party...and I saw this angelic young dolly across the room... And she was looking at me...*gazing* at me, with an expression of rapture in her peerless eyes...and she wandered across to me, and addressed herself to me, and attached herself to me... And plied me with drinks and innocent flattery...and lured me upstairs to some remote bedroom...and there... And there she turned to me with radiant face, parted lips, melting eyes and heaving breast...and unbuttoned her dress with trembling fingers... And drew me down on to the bed, and stroked my hair, and whispered in my ear, murmuring her demure desire and then stuffed her tit in my mouth and her hand down my trousers... (*Pause, then brisk.*) I believe I might succumb. Yes...I might well concede the day there, and might even concede the night.
  (*MRS ELLIOT continues busily tidying up.*)

MRS ELLIOT: (*Disgustedly.*) You *are* sick.

MR ELLIOT: Because I voiced a normal masculine fantasy?

MRS ELLIOT: Because you feel it.

MR ELLIOT: We're trained to feel it, aren't we? From the cradle? Right through adolescence we're encouraged to cultivate our erotic fantasies, to compete in sexual prowess...we're constantly nudged by sexual innuendo and edged toward the marriage bed...and then...and then what happens? The women preoccupy themselves with home-making and child-rearing and the men find consolation in fantasy... As I said, the old ones vent their frustrations in dirty jokes.

MRS ELLIOT: And the young ones go to the clubs?

MR ELLIOT: Yes…but only to look.

MRS ELLIOT: Are they cowards too?

MR ELLIOT: They're faithful.

MRS ELLIOT: Like you.

(*Pause. MR ELLIOT wipes his nose with a handkerchief.*)

MR ELLIOT: You don't believe me, do you?

MRS ELLIOT: Huh.

MR ELLIOT: If we discount the odd bit of self-abuse, and I assume that I am allowed to abuse *myself* if nobody else, I have been faithful to you in my rather reluctant fashion. (*Pause. Then grim.*) My problem is that I am not content to look. (*Pause.*) I don't want to turn into a voyeur.

(*Pause. MRS ELLIOT starts cleaning up.*)

Did I tell you that the boys have clubbed together to buy a film projector and they meet once a week to watch blue movies?

MRS ELLIOT: (*Stops working, stares.*) Blue movies?

MR ELLIOT: (*Explanatory.*) Sex films.

MRS ELLIOT: I didn't think you meant weepies. I know what they are.

MR ELLIOT: Oh really?

MRS ELLIOT: Who goes?

MR ELLIOT: They all go.

MRS ELLIOT: Do you?

MR ELLIOT: I've been twice.

MRS ELLIOT: Do you enjoy them?

MR ELLIOT: No.

MRS ELLIOT: Why? Why not? Aren't the films sexy enough?

MR ELLIOT: I don't mind the films. I don't like the company.

MRS ELLIOT: I thought they were your friends?

MR ELLIOT: They are…individually. But I don't like the 'all-boys-together' atmosphere. (*Pause.*) It's like the whole First Eleven sitting masturbating in the locker room.

(*Pause.*) I'd prefer a mixed audience but they won't dream of it.

MRS ELLIOT: Mixed? What...have a few girls along and an orgy to follow?

MR ELLIOT: (*Laughs.*) That's an idea. But...no, I think a mixed audience would be healthier.

MRS ELLIOT: (*Disbelieving.*) Healthier?

MR ELLIOT: Yes, healthier.

MRS ELLIOT: Why?

MR ELLIOT: (*Impatient.*) It's all tied up with what I was saying before...the masculinity bit...the furtive voyeurism...the morality of the Northern Hero. (*Pause.*) They're all faithful. By Christ they're faithful! (*Silence.*)

MRS ELLIOT: Where do they meet...to see the films?

MR ELLIOT: Harry's.

MRS ELLIOT: (*Amazed.*) What?

MR ELLIOT: Harry's house. (*Silence.*)

MRS ELLIOT: What about his wife?

MR ELLIOT: She goes to her mother's.

MRS ELLIOT: Does she know?

MR ELLIOT: That's why she goes to her mother's. (*Silence.*) Do you mind my going?

MRS ELLIOT: You can do what you like. (*MRS ELLIOT finishes tidying up. She looks round the room, pats down part of the wallpaper, surveys it again.*) I think it'll look nice when everything's back in place. (*MR ELLIOT grunts.*) I think I'll go to bed. (*Pause.*) There's some cheese there if you want a sandwich.

(*MR ELLIOT doesn't reply. She moves toward the door. Then she goes into the kitchen and takes two parcels from the cupboard. She comes back in. Holds them up.*)

Happy Birthday.

MR ELLIOT: Huh.

MRS ELLIOT: They're going to surprise you in the morning.

MR ELLIOT: (*Heavy.*) Tony's going to surprise me with a shaving mirror and Sarah's going to surprise me with a scarf.

MRS ELLIOT: You know?

MR ELLIOT: They've been going on about it for weeks!

MRS ELLIOT: They've been looking forward to it for weeks. (*She puts the parcels down on the table and moves to the door to go.*)

MR ELLIOT: I think it would be healthier if we separated.

MRS ELLIOT: What?

MR ELLIOT: I think we ought to separate.

(*MRS ELLIOT, stunned, moves near the wallpaper.*)

I don't suppose you remember the agreement we had...before we got married...that if ever either of us decided it had been a mistake to marry, we could always separate and then arrange a divorce?

(*MRS ELLIOT stares in silence.*)

Do you remember that agreement?

MRS ELLIOT: That was if there was only you and me.

MR ELLIOT: What?

MRS ELLIOT: Now we've got the children to think of...

MR ELLIOT: That was the agreement we made about marriage.

MRS ELLIOT: And then we had the children...

MR ELLIOT: What about the agreement?

MRS ELLIOT: That doesn't apply!

MR ELLIOT: It applies as much as ever!

MRS ELLIOT: Not with the children!

MR ELLIOT: You never mentioned children.

MRS ELLIOT: Neither did you.

MR ELLIOT: Christ... First you blackmailed me, now you're trapping me.

MRS ELLIOT: (*Indignant.*) Blackmailed?

MR ELLIOT: Yes...as you well know.

MRS ELLIOT: You made your own decision.

MR ELLIOT: Even after we made that agreement... I was still reluctant. And when I suggested that we leave it for a year or so, until we knew each other better...before committing ourselves...when I suggested that, you threatened to commit suicide.

MRS ELLIOT: I did hell!

MR ELLIOT: (*Strained.*) You said...quite simply...that if I didn't go through with the marriage you would kill yourself.

93

MRS ELLIOT: I did not!

MR ELLIOT: I remember the day you said it.

MRS ELLIOT: YOU LYING GET! (*Silence.*)

MR ELLIOT: As a matter of fact I remember talking it over with Harry. I asked his advice. I remember asking him whether he thought a suicide threat would form a good foundation for a happy and lasting relationship. (*Pause.*) He seemed a bit dubious.

MRS ELLIOT: Oh...did he?

MR ELLIOT: Yes...but he wouldn't commit himself.

MRS ELLIOT: Wouldn't he?

MR ELLIOT: I suppose it was a bit much to ask. (*Silence.*)

MRS ELLIOT: You've come out with some lies tonight... about my father and his jokes...and my birth...and your being faithful...and the blue films...but now...now you're excelling yourself!

MR ELLIOT: You prefer not to remember?

MRS ELLIOT: (*High-pitched.*) It didn't happen!

MR ELLIOT: It was about ten days before we were due to get married. I distinctly remember talking it over with Harry.

MRS ELLIOT: I'll ask him!

MR ELLIOT: Go ahead.

MRS ELLIOT: You lying bastard.

MR ELLIOT: I don't need to lie about that...

MRS ELLIOT: I *will* ask him...

MR ELLIOT: That's up to you.

(*MRS ELLIOT goes to the telephone. She throws books aside and looks through an address book by the phone.*)

He's probably in bed now.

MRS ELLIOT: Then I'll get him up.

MR ELLIOT: That'll please him.

MRS ELLIOT: (*Sobbing.*) I'm sick of your lies...

MR ELLIOT: Why don't you ask him tomorrow?

MRS ELLIOT: (*Shrill.*) I'M ASKING HIM NOW!

(*MR ELLIOT shrugs, looks away. Picks up the paperbacks. MRS ELLIOT kneels by the phone with the book. Dials. The answer is immediate. MR ELLIOT glances at her as she speaks.*)

Oh hello…Harry…Harry…this is Norma…Norma
Elliot… I'm sorry it's so late…but… (*Sobbing.*) …Frank
and I…Frank and I…we've been talking…about before
we…er…before we got married and, Frank…I'm
sorry…yes, before we got married… Yes, I KNOW IT'S
HIS BIRTHDAY! All right, I'll tell him, yes, I'll tell
him about the card, all right, never mind…GOD! (*Pause.*)
It's all right…I'm a bit…yes… Frank says I threatened to
commit suicide if he didn't go through with the marriage
and he says he talked it over with you a few days before
the marriage – do you remember? Do you remember
him saying that, Harry? (*Sobbing.*) He says I said I was
going to kill myself unless…what? (*Pause.*) You don't?
No…no…I didn't say it…I didn't say anything like
that… No, that's all right…I'm sorry…it's all right…
(*MR ELLIOT looks at her from across the room.*)

MR ELLIOT: All right…he doesn't remember.

MRS ELLIOT: He didn't say that.

MR ELLIOT: Eh?

MRS ELLIOT: (*Shrieks.*) He said it never happened!

MR ELLIOT: He didn't want to upset you.

MRS ELLIOT: You lying bastard!

MR ELLIOT: I am not lying.

MRS ELLIOT: You're always lying!

MR ELLIOT: (*Violent.*) I'm trying to be honest! Christ, this
is driving me nuts. I'm sick of it. All the bloody
hypocrisy and the lies and the agonies…I'm sick of
them! I'm sick of fantasy…I want reality!

MRS ELLIOT: (*Sarcastic.*) Reality! What reality?

MR ELLIOT: (*Desperately.*) I have to get out of this trap. I
can't stand it. I want to live, to grow, to stretch, to
thrive…I want to be free!

MRS ELLIOT: Free for what?

MR ELLIOT: I want to fuck a thousand women!
(*MR ELLIOT stares furiously around the room. Turns toward
the wallpaper.*)
This house…it's dead. There's no life in it, no life at all.
And this room…white, all white…it's all cold and sterile

and lifeless! There's no love in this room or in this house. NO LOVE! It's DEAD!

(*MR ELLIOT plucks at a little strip of wallpaper that is hanging loose. It peels away, slowly, in his hand. He stares at it fascinated as it peels away. Then he suddenly tears at it and the whole strip peels off the wall, revealing the orange paper underneath. As if berserk, he tears at the next strip. MRS ELLIOT tries to stop him but he pushes her away and tears at the wallpaper, shouting, 'DEAD DEAD DEAD!'. MRS ELLIOT leans sobbing, exhausted against the table. Then she takes the parcels and goes toward the door. MR ELLIOT stops and looks at her.*)

(*Shouts.*) I hate this house and I hate you and I hate the brats!

(*He seizes the parcels. One contains a shaving mirror. He hurls it to the floor and stamps on it.*)

MRS ELLIOT: (*Crying.*) The presents! Stop it! Oh God... you're insane! You're insane!

(*She tries to stop him then she rushes upstairs. MR ELLIOT follows to the door.*)

MR ELLIOT: (*Shouts after her.*) I hate the brats and I hate you!

(*He comes back in. He stamps again on the mirror, then tears open the parcel containing the scarf. He goes to tear the scarf, then lets it slip to the floor. He stares at it, then suddenly moans and sobs. He pulls out a handkerchief and cries.*)

Curtain.

ACT TWO
Pseudomorph

Late Saturday morning in Spring, 1966. The lounge is full of sunshine. There is now a bookcase crammed with books.

MR ELLIOT is heard singing upstairs.

MRS ELLIOT steps from the kitchen and listens. She looks as if she has been crying but is now building up an angry mood. She goes back into the kitchen.

MR ELLIOT comes downstairs into the lounge. He is wearing sky blue flared slacks and his pyjama jacket. He has just had a bath and is rubbing his hair with a towel. He sings loudly, with frequent trills and flourishes.

MR ELLIOT: 'O, O, Antonio,
> He's gone away,
> Left me on my own-io,
> All on my own, you know,
> I'd like to catch him,
> With his new sweetheart,
> And up would go Antonio
> And his ice-cream cart!'
> (*He stands in front of a wall mirror and combs his hair, experimenting with various styles: flat back like Valentino (he particularly admires this), flat forward over his eyes, centre parted like an old footballer, and completely free and uncombed...*
> *MRS ELLIOT steps from the kitchen and watches him sourly.*
> *MR ELLIOT prances before the mirror, in high spirits, squinting at his profile, winking archly at himself, laughing.*
> *MRS ELLIOT steps forward. She is holding a wet frying-pan. MR ELLIOT sees her in the mirror. He laughs and speaks into the mirror.*)
> What is it? Breakfast or battery?
> (*MRS ELLIOT steps toward him. He laughs but moves away.*)
> You wouldn't attack a man in his pyjamas?

MRS ELLIOT: Where did *you* go last night?

MR ELLIOT: Out.

MRS ELLIOT: Where to?

MR ELLIOT: I disremember.

(*Pause. MRS ELLIOT stands staring at him angrily.*)

MRS ELLIOT: WHERE DID YOU GET TO?

MR ELLIOT: I went boozing and whoring around as usual.

(*Pause. He moves back to the mirror and resumes combing his hair, now serious.*)

MRS ELLIOT: Were you with that slut?

MR ELLIOT: Which slut?

MRS ELLIOT: You know *which slut*!

MR ELLIOT: You know…your tone is as limited as your diction. (*Pause.*) I don't know which slut. (*Then flip.*) She's just one in a thousand…

MRS ELLIOT: I'll swing for her yet!

MR ELLIOT: Nobody…*swings* in this civilized society.

MRS ELLIOT: Filthy little slut!

MR ELLIOT: Oh…for Christ's sake…

(*He stares at her in the mirror for a moment. She goes back into the kitchen. Then he combs his hair, and sings.*)

'I'd like to catch him

With his dum de da,

And up would go who you know

In his da de da!'

MRS ELLIOT: (*From kitchen.*) Will you tell your slut to keep her filth out of the car?

MR ELLIOT: Eh?

MRS ELLIOT: Tell her to keep her filth out of the car.

MR ELLIOT: Oh…what filth?

MRS ELLIOT: HER FILTH!

(*MR ELLIOT glances around, then back to the mirror.*)

MR ELLIOT: O… O… Anto…nio…

(*MRS ELLIOT comes out, goes to a drawer.*)

MRS ELLIOT: And give her this.

(*MR ELLIOT turns.*

MRS ELLIOT flicks a small tube at him. He picks it up.)

MR ELLIOT: What?

MRS ELLIOT: You know what.

MR ELLIOT: You seem to think I'm...omniscient.

MRS ELLIOT: FILTH!

MR ELLIOT: Eyeshadow! (*Then with sad irony.*) I thought her eyes were beautiful! (*Pause. Sarcastically.*) So...you've been cleaning the car, have you?

MRS ELLIOT: No...that's your job.

MR ELLIOT: Oh...

MRS ELLIOT: That's a job for you.

MR ELLIOT: (*A little puzzled.*) Oh yes...we must have the family saloon polished and gleaming for this afternoon, mustn't we?

MRS ELLIOT: (*Laughs.*) Huh!

(*MR ELLIOT stares at her, worried by her manner.*)

MR ELLIOT: (*Straightforward.*) What's so funny?

MRS ELLIOT: You dirtied it...you clean it.

(*MR ELLIOT goes through the kitchen to the garage.
MRS ELLIOT tidies up. Puts a child's bicycle in garden.
Goes to kitchen. MR ELLIOT storms back in.*)

MR ELLIOT: (*Blustering.*) Stupid bitch! What good does that do?

MRS ELLIOT: What?

MR ELLIOT: You've scrawled all over the car!

MRS ELLIOT: I haven't 'scrawled all over the car'...

MR ELLIOT: You've scratched the body!

MRS ELLIOT: (*Vicious glee.*) I wrote 'SLUT' on the bonnet.

MR ELLIOT: ...and scraped the paintwork. Cost a fortune to repair. You can't just...*wash*...that stuff off, you know.

MRS ELLIOT: Leave it the way it is.

MR ELLIOT: Yes...that's an idea. (*Pause.*) It'll be a bit of a diversion at School Sports Day...for the parents and teachers, I mean. They can while away the afternoon discussing who Mr Elliot's slut is, and forget about their brats.

(*MR ELLIOT sits down and hurls the towel across the room,
just missing MRS ELLIOT. She picks it up.
She sits on the couch, looking at him from the side.*)

In fact, you couldn't have chosen a better way of publicising our...arrangement.

MRS ELLIOT: You don't have to go to the Sports Day.

MR ELLIOT: You've been on about it all week!

MRS ELLIOT: We can easily walk there and back...

MR ELLIOT: Throughout the week you have *repeatedly* asseverated that the success of our brats in the athletics depended *totally* on my inspiring presence. In fact...in fact you made it clear that if I was not present then Sarah would break her neck in the Long Jump and Tony would set fire to the Entertainments Tent!

MRS ELLIOT: Where do you go?

MR ELLIOT: What?

MRS ELLIOT: Where do you go?

MR ELLIOT: Where do I go where?

MRS ELLIOT: With her?

MR ELLIOT: Oh hell...

MRS ELLIOT: Where do you go? (*Voice rising.*) Do you go to...the Promenade at Otterspool? (*Pause.*) Or Sefton Park? Or is that too public? (*Pause.*) Or do you drive down behind the warehouses in the Dock Road? (*Pause.*) Where do you go with her?

MR ELLIOT: (*Flat.*) We sit and shag in the middle of Lime Street. (*Pause.*)

MRS ELLIOT: Are you still seeing her?

MR ELLIOT: Who?

MRS ELLIOT: YOU KNOW WHO!

MR ELLIOT: You keep saying that! (*Mocking.*) 'You know who you know who you know who...' I don't. I don't know!

MRS ELLIOT: Your slut.

MR ELLIOT: (*Polite inquiry.*) You mean Eileen?
(*The expression of the name has a shock effect on MRS ELLIOT, who trembles with anger and struggles for self-control.*
MR ELLIOT sits tense but composed.
Long silence.)

MRS ELLIOT: It's funny...

MR ELLIOT: What?

MRS ELLIOT: All your sluts... (*Pause.*) Maur*een*...Dor*een* ...J*ean*...Eil*een*...

MR ELLIOT: (*Smiling.*) Yes...they all share the same ending. (*He howls with laughter; then smiling.*) I made a joke...

MRS ELLIOT: (*Sourly.*) You ought to write a poem about them.

MR ELLIOT: I could just as easily write a poem about Dora...Vera...Brenda... (*Pause.*) My mother was much preoccupied with names. She had them all classified. Good names like...Helen. Phoney names like...Shirley. Ugly names like Edna. (*Pause.*) It's a primitive obsession. Are you going nuts?

MRS ELLIOT: Is that surprising?

MR ELLIOT: You always were a bit weird.
(*Long pause. MR ELLIOT moves to get up from the chair.*)

MRS ELLIOT: I want to know.

MR ELLIOT: What? (*Long pause.*) You want to know WHAT?

MRS ELLIOT: Are you still seeing her?

MR ELLIOT: (*Considered.*) No.
(*MRS ELLIOT stares hard at him from the side. He stares toward the garden.*)

MRS ELLIOT: Swear...

MR ELLIOT: (*Mocking: child's voice.*) Cross my heart and swear to die...

MRS ELLIOT: (*Very tense.*) I want you to swear.

MR ELLIOT: (*Chuckles.*) All right, all right.

MRS ELLIOT: Do you swear you're not still seeing her?

MR ELLIOT: I swear whatever you like...

MRS ELLIOT: DO YOU SWEAR? YOU'RE NOT SEEING HER?

MR ELLIOT: (*Flatly.*) I swear.
(*Pause. MRS ELLIOT leans forward toward him.*)

MRS ELLIOT: (*Disbelieving.*) Swear...on your mother's grave?

MR ELLIOT: (*Explodes.*) OH! For Christ's sake!
(*He jumps up. She grabs his sleeve. He stops.*)

MRS ELLIOT: Swear on your mother's grave...

MR ELLIOT: (*Heavily and as if on the stand.*) I swear on my mother's grave that I am not seeing her.

MRS ELLIOT: (*Eagerly.*) ...Eileen...

(*MR ELLIOT groans and delicately releases her hold on his sleeve, almost in slow motion.*)

MR ELLIOT: (*Witness-box tone again.*) I swear on my mother's grave that I am not seeing Eileen.

(*MRS ELLIOT sits back in the couch, tight-lipped. MR ELLIOT looks down at her. Silence.*)

Why...*why*...do you focus your vindictiveness on her? Her...out of a thousand? Why her?

MRS ELLIOT: Because I know who she is.

MR ELLIOT: (*Surprised.*) Oh...you've been cleaning my suits again, have you?

MRS ELLIOT: She'll pay...

MR ELLIOT: What?

MRS ELLIOT: She'll pay!

MR ELLIOT: (*Softly.*) Even if I'm not seeing her?

MRS ELLIOT: (*Harsh.*) Aren't you?

MR ELLIOT: CHRIST! (*Long pause.*) You know...the real issue here...the real thing at issue... is which one of us is going to go nuts first. Or rather, which one of us is going to go nuts last. (*Laughs.*) Last to go nuts goes free!

MRS ELLIOT: Huh...that's no problem. You're never going free.

MR ELLIOT: Who wants to 'go' free? I'm free now.

MRS ELLIOT: Are you?

MR ELLIOT: And I'm quite satisfied with our arrangement.

(*He goes to the kitchen and brings out an ironing-board. Plugs the iron into a socket. Fetches shirts from a basket in the hail. Begins ironing. MRS ELLIOT sits watching.*)

(*Ironing an orange shirt. Speaks in reasonable tones but with an underlying bite.*) Our arrangement does still...stand, I take it? (*Pause.*) You do accept the terms we agreed... don't you?

(*He stops and looks at MRS ELLIOT, who looks away. He shrugs, speaks quietly.*)

I don't mind whether I live *here*...or on my own, somewhere. It makes no difference to me. So...if you want me to live here...if you *still* want me to stay here with you and the kids, I'm quite willing to do so. (*Pause. Then sharp.*) As long as you don't interfere with my private life. (*Studies MRS ELLIOT; she ignores him.*) We did agree, didn't we, that I should continue to live here, paying the mortgage and insurance bills on the property, every month...and the gas and electricity and telephone bills every quarter...and the rates every year...plus, of course, adequate housekeeping money every week?

MRS ELLIOT: HUH!

MR ELLIOT: (*Sour look.*) In other words, we agreed, didn't we, that I should devote my total income to the upkeep of the family, and live...*live*...on, or rather OFF, my overdraft? And of course, I should do all my own shopping and cooking and laundry? (*Pause.*) In return for which, you would not interfere with my *private* life... Agreed? (*He stops and looks at MRS ELLIOT.*) We did agree, didn't we...? (*She looks sourly at him.*) On those terms we agreed to carry on with this mockery of a marriage...which is to say, this mockery of a mockery...

MRS ELLIOT: Do you know how ridiculous you look in those trousers?

MR ELLIOT: What?

MRS ELLIOT: You heard.

MR ELLIOT: My sailor pants? (*Coy.*) I think they're very fetching.

MRS ELLIOT: All you need now is beads and sandals.

MR ELLIOT: (*Light.*) And whiskers...

(*Pause.*)

MRS ELLIOT: You're not going dressed like that, are you?

MR ELLIOT: Why not?

MRS ELLIOT: At School Sports?

MR ELLIOT: Why not?

MRS ELLIOT: (*Derisive.*) They'll all take you for one of the Sixth Form!

MR ELLIOT: I'll make a few schoolgirl hearts flutter...

MRS ELLIOT: You'll make yourself a laughing stock!

MR ELLIOT: (*Wounded.*) What do you want me to wear?

MRS ELLIOT: Anything suitable for your age…if you've got anything.

MR ELLIOT: (*Angry.*) White shirt and pullover and grey flannels?

MRS ELLIOT: Whatever you like.

MR ELLIOT: All right, all right!

(*He snatches a white shirt from the pile, holds it up and begins to iron, furiously.*)

MRS ELLIOT: And when are you going to get Sarah her School Uniform?

MR ELLIOT: She doesn't *have* to have a School Uniform.

MRS ELLIOT: (*Bitter.*) She'll be the only child there without one this afternoon. (*Pause.*) Anyway…you promised her one.

MR ELLIOT: Oh…did I?

MRS ELLIOT: You did… (*Biting.*) Eighteen months ago.

MR ELLIOT: In that case I have broken my promise…

MRS ELLIOT: Yes!

MR ELLIOT: …which will confirm Sarah in the opinion of me that you are carefully cultivating.

MRS ELLIOT: (*Sour.*) I don't *need* to cultivate it!

MR ELLIOT: Do you ever stop to consider the effect your raving has on the child? Your raving about men, in general…and me, in particular? (*Pause.*) She'll turn queer…

MRS ELLIOT: She might be better off at that.

MR ELLIOT: Christ…don't tell me you're developing reservations about marriage too?

MRS ELLIOT: I always did have reservations about marriage… (*Long silence. MR ELLIOT irons away.*) Was she a virgin?

MR ELLIOT: Who? (*Then quickly.*) Don't say it – 'my slut'!

MRS ELLIOT: Was she?

MR ELLIOT: (*Sings.*) 'She said she was a virgin
But alas she spoke too soon!'

MRS ELLIOT: Sometimes I'm sorry for her. (*Pause.*) You're really sick. You're really a sick, randy, adolescent Peter Pan.

MR ELLIOT: (*Cheerful.*) Skip the Peter – just call me Pan!
(*Pause.*)
Your only real grievance is that I'm randy and successful.
(*MR ELLIOT carries on ironing.*
After a while he stops and looks at MRS ELLIOT.)
Why *did* you marry me then?

MRS ELLIOT: I was sorry for you.

MR ELLIOT: Huh!

MRS ELLIOT: I didn't...really...want to get married. I'd
seen the girls at work crowing over their brand new gold
rings...and I'd seen them a year later, living in broken-
down flats, with a baby at the breast and another on the
way...and sick of it all. When I met you I was old
enough to know the difference between a wedding and a
marriage! (*Pause.*) That was why I hadn't got married...
before. (*Pause.*) I didn't want children. I don't want
children now. (*Then ironic.*) But as they say in the
magazines, when you have them you love them. (*Then
bitter.*) You haven't got much choice. (*Pause.*) I worry
about Tony sometimes. He's got exactly the same wild,
coltish quality you had...before you hardened.

MR ELLIOT: *Me?* Hard?

MRS ELLIOT: Yes...you've grown hard with people as
you've grown weak with yourself. You always were
weak...you've grown weaker.

MR ELLIOT: And...like they say in the magazines...
I suppose it was my weakness that won you?

MRS ELLIOT: Yes.
(*Long pause. MR ELLIOT returns determinedly to his ironing.*)

MR ELLIOT: (*Sings harshly.*) 'IF ANY YOUNG LADY WANTS A
BABY, COME TO THE COCK OF THE NORTH!'
(*MRS ELLIOT stares at him for a while.*)

MRS ELLIOT: Do they know you're married?

MR ELLIOT: Who?

MRS ELLIOT: These...little sluts...you pick up in the
clubs...

MR ELLIOT: They can see my fingernails.
(*MR ELLIOT goes upstairs.*

MRS ELLIOT crosses to the ironing-board and looks at the shirts. She sits down again.
MR ELLIOT returns with a pair of grey trousers and begins to iron them.)

You're not going like that, are you?

MRS ELLIOT: Eh?

MR ELLIOT: You're not going to Sports Day dressed like that, are you?

MRS ELLIOT: (*A bit defensive.*) Why...

MR ELLIOT: You look like an old shrew.

MRS ELLIOT: That's not surprising!

MR ELLIOT: You don't have to *look* the part.

MRS ELLIOT: (*Voice rising.*) And what else have I got to wear? I got *this* dress two years ago... (*Shrill.*) ...one of my sister's cast-offs!

MR ELLIOT: (*Brutal.*) That's because you're a bloody awful housekeeper.

MRS ELLIOT: (*Aghast.*) WHAT?
(*She rushes to a sideboard, produces an exercise book and pushes it in front of MR ELLIOT. He refuses to look at it.*)
Last week...four pounds three shillings housekeeping. Four pounds to feed a family!

MR ELLIOT: You don't feed *me.*

MRS ELLIOT: You use tea, and milk, and sugar...where do they come from? Look at the week before...three pounds eighteen!

MR ELLIOT: (*Grins.*) It's the end of the month.

MRS ELLIOT: Every week's the end of the month with you!

MR ELLIOT: You'd be better off if you let me separate.

MRS ELLIOT: HUH! If I can't get the money when you're here...

MR ELLIOT: You'd get your money.

MRS ELLIOT: How much do you give her?

MR ELLIOT: (*Mechanical.*) Who?

MRS ELLIOT: YOUR SLUT!

MR ELLIOT: Give her?

MRS ELLIOT: Why else should she go with you? With an old man?

MR ELLIOT: Because I'm sexy and handsome.

MRS ELLIOT: HUH!

MR ELLIOT: If you want to know, she often used to help me out. Because...often...I was broke. (*Pause, then bitter.*) Which is not all that surprising, considering what it costs to maintain you and the brats!

MRS ELLIOT: (*Looking sourly at his clothes.*) I bet they cost a few pounds.

MR ELLIOT: Which I earned.

MRS ELLIOT: What?

MR ELLIOT: (*Hard.*) They cost a few pounds...which I EARNED!

(*Long pause. MR ELLIOT irons.*)

MRS ELLIOT: You borrowed the money off your father. (*MR ELLIOT is surprised but ignores this. Pause.*) You'd better pay him back, hadn't you...before it's too late?

MR ELLIOT: He's not...on his death-bed yet, you know. (*Then heated.*) He's the only thing that keeps me here! (*Pause.*) Apart from the fact that I can't afford the price of a suitcase! (*Turns to MRS ELLIOT.*) Why don't you get a job?

MRS ELLIOT: What?

MR ELLIOT: You rant on about being short of money... why don't you get a job?

MRS ELLIOT: To subsidize your whoring?

MR ELLIOT: (*Despairing.*) Ahhhh.

(*Long pause. MR ELLIOT stops ironing.*)

It's crazy. I owe my father money.

MRS ELLIOT: (*Shrill.*) You owe *me* money!

MR ELLIOT: (*Heavily.*) I owe *you* money. I owe my friends money. I owe my employers money. I owe the bank money. (*Pause.*) Christ, I must owe *myself* money! (*Pause; muttering to himself.*) I owe myself something, anyway. (*Pause; then, turning, points to MRS ELLIOT.*) Why the hell do we stay together? (*She ignores him.*) You are my poison ivy, I am your wall, da de da... (*Pause.*) We're held together by a string of...mini-bonds...that mean precisely nothing! Why? (*Then measured.*) I think I would like a divorce after all.

MRS ELLIOT: (*Quickly.*) You've no grounds for divorce.

MR ELLIOT: I've got the only grounds for divorce... I'm *married*! (*Pause.*) This...arrangement...of ours...won't work. It's a shell within a shell. And it won't work, because you won't allow it to. You say you will, but in fact you insist on...*hounding* me! And the hypocrisy of it is driving me nuts! (*Pause.*)

MRS ELLIOT: I suppose you think you're in love with *her*?

MR ELLIOT: (*Theatrical.*) Yes! Madly! Madly in love! When she breathes in, I breathe out!

MRS ELLIOT: But you don't see her...

MR ELLIOT: *There* you go again... (*Pause; takes a dictionary from a bookshelf and points out a word.*) You know...when a structure has lost its essence but retained its shape, the geologists call it: a Pseudomorph. A false shape. (*Pause.*) That's our marriage...a false shape: a Pseudomorph.

MRS ELLIOT: Very neat.

MR ELLIOT: (*Resigned.*) Thank you. (*Then as if making an announcement.*) 'The marriage survived and the partners quietly withered.' Christ! I want us to look forward to a Silver Divorce! I can't live this way! (*Turns to her; harsh.*) Why can't you go out and get yourself poked by some great hairy male...

MRS ELLIOT: (*Light.*) ...to ease your conscience?

MR ELLIOT: (*Raving.*) ...to cure your obsession with me! To stop you hounding me! I'm not the man you want but you insist on trying to *make* me what you want. You want me to be a good paterfamilias and I am *not* a good paterfamilias and I don't *want* to be a good paterfamilias! I want to be...*me*. I don't want to be 'Mr Elliot of Greengate Avenue' ...I want to be me! I want to live...live *my* way of life. I want...JOY!

MRS ELLIOT: But you *are* Mr Elliot of Greengate Avenue...

MR ELLIOT: I *hate* Mr Elliot!

MRS ELLIOT: (*Laughs.*) You're mad.

MR ELLIOT: I'm heading in that direction. (*He sits. Pause. Then pleading.*) Why can't we just agree to live separately... and honestly?

MRS ELLIOT: (*Snaps.*) I MADE YOU! She's not going to get the benefit.

MR ELLIOT: (*Deep frustration.*) Ahhhh.

MRS ELLIOT: Maybe you feel trapped...but don't forget, I'm trapped too.

MR ELLIOT: Okay...we're both trapped. (*Pause.*) You know, it's crazy... Society is organized to create loneliness...the loneliness that leads to marriage. Society creates the disease...then prescribes a worse one as cure. Men enslave women...then wake up to find they've enslaved themselves!

(*Pause.*)

Do we like to torture ourselves? Because that's what we've, so carefully, arranged. (*Then bitterly, incredulous.*) When I was a boy I used to chastise myself...in emulation of the great Catholic masochists...like St John of the Cross. For three weeks I wore a rope of barbed wire round my waist...to mortify the flesh. But after three weeks the flesh began to scream...and I took the rope off. (*Pause.*) Now...now I wear that rope of wire around my brain... (*Hands to head.*) ...it's biting deeper and deeper and deeper...and I *can't* get it off!

(*Long pause.*)

MRS ELLIOT: (*Composed but bitter.*) I'm sick of it too...you know.

MR ELLIOT: Then why hang on to it?

MRS ELLIOT: (*Ignoring him.*) I've *grown* sick of it. I've grown sick of you, and sick of sex, and sick of love. (*Pause.*) I'm sick of all the burning and the fretting and the weeping...I'm sick of the betrayals and sick of the fidelity...I'm sick of the lies and sick of the truth. I want nothing more of it. I am sick of it all.

(*Long pause.*)

MR ELLIOT: Then why...hang on to it?

MRS ELLIOT: Because I've resigned myself to it.

MR ELLIOT: Oh...have you?

MRS ELLIOT: ...and you'll have to resign yourself to it too.

MR ELLIOT: If you've 'resigned' yourself to it...why do you hound me? (*Pause; then violently.*) And why do you hound her?

MRS ELLIOT: Who?

(*Pause.*)

Hound who?

(*Long pause.*)

(*Indignant and suspicious.*) Why do I hound who?

(*MR ELLIOT turns away and busies himself with the ironing. Silence.*)

(*Shrill.*) What did you mean by that?

MR ELLIOT: (*Turns on her.*) Oh...BUGGER OFF!

(*MRS ELLIOT glances at him. Then, composing herself.*)

MRS ELLIOT: I haven't been 'hounding' anyone.

(*MR ELLIOT turns and looks at her. He is provoked but restrained.*)

MR ELLIOT: (*Sarcastic.*) Oh no?

MRS ELLIOT: No.

MR ELLIOT: Haven't you?

MRS ELLIOT: NO!

(*Pause. MR ELLIOT resumes ironing. Silence. Then speaking conversationally, almost indifferently.*)

MR ELLIOT: I heard you had.

MRS ELLIOT: (*Quickly.*) Had what?

MR ELLIOT: I heard you'd been hounding her.

MRS ELLIOT: Who?

MR ELLIOT: Eileen.

MRS ELLIOT: Huh... (*Pause; then tensely.*) How did you hear that?

MR ELLIOT: (*Flat.*) That doesn't matter.

MRS ELLIOT: (*Voice trembling a little.*) How...did you hear?

MR ELLIOT: I heard you'd been telephoning...screaming and raving on the phone. You kept calling her 'slut'. Slut slut slut...

MRS ELLIOT: (*Agitated.*) Have you been seeing her?

MR ELLIOT: It's got to stop! You understand what I mean?

(*He turns and stands confronting MRS ELLIOT.*)

MRS ELLIOT: I didn't telephone!

MR ELLIOT: Then who did?

(*Silence.*)

Somebody telephoned her at work.

(*MRS ELLIOT stares at her hands. She is trembling.*)

MRS ELLIOT: (*Shrill.*) I'm going to make that little slut pay.

MR ELLIOT: (*Harsh but composed.*) If you try – if you even try – I'll sell this house and send the kids to boarding school.

MRS ELLIOT: (*Quickly.*) You can't do that!

MR ELLIOT: Can't I?

MRS ELLIOT: (*Shrill.*) I DIDN'T TELEPHONE!

MR ELLIOT: (*Bitter.*) Somebody telephoned. (*Pause.*) Somebody telephoned her at work and threatened to tell her family 'what she was'.

MRS ELLIOT: I didn't.

MR ELLIOT: Who then? (*Pause.*) Your sister? (*Silence. Then MR ELLIOT speaks in reasonable tones, appealing to her.*) Look…I know – know how –

MRS ELLIOT: Have you been seeing her?

MR ELLIOT: Will you listen? Her father is ill –

MRS ELLIOT: Have you been seeing her?

MR ELLIOT: (*Shouts.*) YES! YES I HAVE!

MRS ELLIOT: You lying bastard!

MR ELLIOT: (*Very angry.*) Her father is ill – very ill – and if you start –

MRS ELLIOT: (*Trembling, very shrill.*) I knew! I knew you'd been seeing her…

MR ELLIOT: I'm not seeing her now. Her father is very ill –

MRS ELLIOT: I hope he dies in agony!

(*MR ELLIOT slaps her hard across the face. She kicks him. He jumps back, knocking over the ironing-board, and falls with it. As he moves to get up she screeches, kicks him again. He falls, gets up. He tries to punch her, they grapple and thresh round the room in a fury of blows and scratches, knocking over furniture and swearing viciously at each other.*)

*Finally, exhausted, they lie apart, staring at each other. MR
ELLIOT leans against a chair, struggling for breath.*)

MR ELLIOT: Oh Christ...we have got to end this. (*Pause.*)
This Roman Arena...you with your net...and me with
my bloody trident... (*Gasps – laughs.*) And upstairs...the
little Emperor...and the Empress...listening...turning
down thumbs... We have got to *end* this farce. (*Pause; he
moves to get up.*) Right. All right. We'll carry on...for a
bit...with our agreement...all right? And we'll go...to
the Sports...we'll play our parts this afternoon...
(*As he speaks, MRS ELLIOT shudders; her eyes brighten;
and she screeches wildly, piercingly and breaks into a fit of
weird, hysterical non-stop babbling that drowns his speech.*)

MRS ELLIOT: SLUTTYSLUTTYSLUTTYSLUTTY
SLUTTYSLUTTYSLUTTYSLUTTYSLUTTYSLUTTY
SLUTTYSLUTTY.
(*MR ELLIOT stares at her, horrified and frightened as she
babbles on.*)

Curtain.

ACT THREE
Alpha Beta

Summer, 1971. The lounge. Very untidy, poorly decorated, and the furnishing is worn. On a table is a stainless steel tray with three tumblers full of water.

The French window opens on to an overgrown garden. A child's bicycle lies on its side on the grass. It is raining. The time is about 9:00 in the evening and the light is beginning to fade.

MRS ELLIOT sits motionless in an armchair. She wears a shapeless cotton dress.

MR ELLIOT lets himself in the front door and enters. He wears a shiny brown suit and coat, soaked with rain. He looks tired, old and tense.

MR ELLIOT: Hi.
  (*MRS ELLIOT doesn't answer or look at him.*)
  What's the matter?
  (*He sits on the arm of a couch on her left. There is complete silence.*)
  What's the matter?
  (*Silence. He stares at her. She stares ahead.*)
  Where are the kids? (*Pause.*) In bed?
  (*He gets up. Looks at MRS ELLIOT. Then he goes out and upstairs. She remains staring. Re-enters, quietly. Looks relieved.*)
  I didn't wake them.
  (*He stands looking at MRS ELLIOT. She ignores him.*)
  Is your head bad?
  (*Her foot jerks. She ignores it. He stares at her foot. After a long pause her foot jerks again. He looks at her face but she is still staring straight ahead.*)
  Fancy a cup of coffee?
  (*He goes into the kitchen to make the coffee. He looks round the kitchen. It is in a mess.*)

I came as soon as I could. There was a bit of a crisis in
the office. You know…the announcement. Did you hear
the announcement? Seems like the strike's off…for a day
or two, anyway. So for three weeks I'm sitting there
waiting for the phone to ring and today it never stops.
Mind you, I half expected it. As soon as the Government
said they would use troops to lift perishable cargo – that
was a couple of days ago – I knew they'd have to do
something. (*Pause.*) The dockers said they'd handle
perishable cargo for medical supplies, or anything urgent
like that…

(*MR ELLIOT comes back in. Takes the glasses off the tray.
Looks at them for a moment. Leaves them on the table and
takes the tray. Speaks from the kitchen.*)

Some of the calls I've had…they're crazy! They think
because the strike's off they'll have supplies in the shops
tonight! That all I have to do is telephone a few drivers
and the job's done. Deliveries under way! Perishable
cargo…they don't know what the word means.

(*MR ELLIOT comes back with the tray, carrying two coffees
and a plate of biscuits.*)

They wouldn't thank you for fifty thousand bad bananas!

(*He puts the tray down on the floor between the couch and
the armchair. Offers MRS ELLIOT a cup of coffee. She ignores
it. He puts it on the floor. He sits on the couch.*)

Some biscuits there. (*Pause.*) How's your head been?

MRS ELLIOT: My head's been all right.

(*Silence.*)

MR ELLIOT: Oh…good.

(*MRS ELLIOT gets up and goes out, upstairs. MR ELLIOT
sips his coffee. He puts down the coffee and looks critically
round the room. He looks toward the garden and sees the bike
in the rain. Stands by the window and studies the state of the
garden. Then looks again round the room. MRS ELLIOT
comes back and sits in the same place.*)

All right?

MRS ELLIOT: (*Sitting.*) What?

MR ELLIOT: (*Sitting.*) The…the kids?

MRS ELLIOT: I didn't look.

(*Silence. MR ELLIOT studies the stainless steel tray.*)

MR ELLIOT: (*Making conversation.*) You've started using the tray.

MRS ELLIOT: (*Staring ahead.*) Mmmm.

MR ELLIOT: It's a nice tray. Handsome.

MRS ELLIOT: (*Looking at it.*) We might as well use it.

MR ELLIOT: (*Embarrassed.*) Oh yeah...you might as well. It's only going...

MRS ELLIOT: It was going rusty.

MR ELLIOT: Rusty? Really? (*Picks it up and examines it.*) It was supposed to be stainless steel.

MRS ELLIOT: They still *rust.*

MR ELLIOT: Oh...yeah...I suppose so.

MRS ELLIOT: (*Bitterly.*) And it was bought two years ago.

MR ELLIOT: (*Scrutinizing it.*) I know.

MRS ELLIOT: It's underneath.

MR ELLIOT: What?

MRS ELLIOT: (*Snaps.*) The *rust.*

MR ELLIOT: Oh...yeah...I see.

MRS ELLIOT: That was why we decided to use it.

MR ELLIOT: You've cleaned it up...

MRS ELLIOT: You'd look silly giving it to your father now.

MR ELLIOT: Now?

MRS ELLIOT: It was supposed to be a birthday present. (*Bitterly.*) Don't you remember?

MR ELLIOT: (*Guilty.*) Yes.

MRS ELLIOT: He was asking about the job. How it was going.

MR ELLIOT: (*Embarrassed.*) Was he?

MRS ELLIOT: On Saturday.

MR ELLIOT: What did you say?

MRS ELLIOT: I said it was all right...as far as I knew.

MR ELLIOT: Yeah...it's all right. (*Pause.*) Well...the dock strike didn't help. The girls were sitting in the office with nothing to do.

MRS ELLIOT: What about you?

MR ELLIOT: What?

MRS ELLIOT: (*Dry.*) Couldn't *you* keep them occupied?

MR ELLIOT: Me? (*Pause.*) I was in the same boat. (*Laughs mirthlessly.*) I made a joke. (*Pause.*) Your coffee will be cold.

(*MRS ELLIOT very deliberately picks up the coffee and sips it.*)

(*Defensive.*) How was he?

MRS ELLIOT: (*Making him say it.*) Who?

MR ELLIOT: My father.

MRS ELLIOT: (*Level.*) He had a cold.

MR ELLIOT: (*Concerned.*) Oh...

MRS ELLIOT: He hadn't been out for two days. He stayed in bed.

MR ELLIOT: (*Approving.*) Yeah...that was sensible. That's the best thing to do with a cold.

MRS ELLIOT: He looks after himself.

MR ELLIOT: He's stronger than you think.

MRS ELLIOT: (*Snaps.*) How would you know?

MR ELLIOT: All I meant was... He's basically a *strong* man...sound...he's got a sound constitution...and good reserves of strength...

MRS ELLIOT: He's old.

MR ELLIOT: He's not old!

MRS ELLIOT: What is he then?

MR ELLIOT: He's only...sixty... (*Lamely.*) ...sixty-seven.

MRS ELLIOT: I suppose you think that's young?

MR ELLIOT: Well...I'm not saying he's *young*...I mean...

(*Pause.*) I mean, he's very strong...for a man of his age.

MRS ELLIOT: You said he wasn't old.

MR ELLIOT: Okay... He's not old for a man of his age.

MRS ELLIOT: No...he's a young sixty-seven.

MR ELLIOT: Well...he *is*.

MRS ELLIOT: Which still does not make him young.

MR ELLIOT: I did not say he was *young*!

MRS ELLIOT: (*Snarls.*) You said he was *not old*.

(*Silence. MR ELLIOT stands decisively. Pause. He stoops and puts the coffee cups on the tray. Hers is unfinished. He proffers it, she ignores him. Walks toward the kitchen. Stops by the table to put the three glasses on the tray.*)

(*Sharp.*) Leave them there.

MR ELLIOT: What?

MRS ELLIOT: Leave them there.

(*MR ELLIOT scrutinizes the glasses. Goes to take a sip. Snaps warning.*) Leave it alone!

MR ELLIOT: (*Puzzled and annoyed.*) What is it? Lemonade?

MRS ELLIOT: Just leave the glasses there.

MR ELLIOT: Is it water?

MRS ELLIOT: (*Hard.*) Yes.

MR ELLIOT: There's more in the tap, isn't there? It looks untidy. (*Sarcastic.*) Or doesn't it bother you?

MRS ELLIOT: About as much as it bothers you.

(*MR ELLIOT flinches. Then he goes into the kitchen, leaving the glasses on the table.*
MRS ELLIOT sits motionless, staring toward the garden, while he washes up.)

MR ELLIOT: (*Shouts from kitchen.*) THIS KITCHEN LOOKS A DUMP! (*He comes back in. Starts clearing up tea table.*) Why don't you clean it up?

MRS ELLIOT: Why don't you?

MR ELLIOT: That's your job.

MRS ELLIOT: HUH!

MR ELLIOT: It *is* your job.

MRS ELLIOT: It's your kitchen. You clean it up.

MR ELLIOT: You *are* supposed to be the housewife round here, aren't you?

MRS ELLIOT: And you're supposed to be the househusband...'round here'...aren't you?

MR ELLIOT: I'm not talking about that.

MRS ELLIOT: Oh no...you wouldn't be!

MR ELLIOT: (*Heavy control.*) I'm simply referring to the fact that you have no obligations...no duties...no tasks...no responsibilities...in a word, no JOB...beyond that of running this household, i.e. looking after the children and maintaining the property in good order...and, in the circumstances, you might reasonably be expected to do more than sit on your fanny all day staring into space!

MRS ELLIOT: (*Vicious mimicry.*) 'Maintain the property in good order...'

117

MR ELLIOT: Yes.

MRS ELLIOT: (*Jeering.*) You're more worried about the property than you are about the children!

MR ELLIOT: (*At the door.*) What? What does that mean?

MRS ELLIOT: (*Full flood.*) You and your property! Are you worried about the price you'll get? Is that what's worrying you?

MR ELLIOT: (*Baffled.*) I don't get you...

MRS ELLIOT: No, but I get you! I get you well!

MR ELLIOT: What are you on about?

MRS ELLIOT: You're going to sell the house and throw us into the street!

MR ELLIOT: You mean into the avenue.

MRS ELLIOT: Just try it! Just try it!

MR ELLIOT: You don't really think that.

MRS ELLIOT: You don't know what I think.

MR ELLIOT: You just *want* to think it.

MRS ELLIOT: You said you would.

MR ELLIOT: (*Suddenly wearily.*) I said I would what?

MRS ELLIOT: You said you'd sell the house.

MR ELLIOT: I...threatened...to sell the house.

MRS ELLIOT: Huh! Threatened!

MR ELLIOT: Yes...I *threatened* to sell the house. (*Pause.*) You forced me to.

MRS ELLIOT: Don't blame me for what you've done.

MR ELLIOT: (*More excited.*) *You* were threatening *me*!

MRS ELLIOT: (*Sarcastic.*) *Me* threatening *you*? Ahhhh... poor babby!

MR ELLIOT: You said you were going to make me pay.

MRS ELLIOT: (*Bitter.*) Her pay.

MR ELLIOT: What?

MRS ELLIOT: I said I was going to make *her* pay. (*Silence. MRS ELLIOT turns to look at him. Then intensely.*) Your slut.

MR ELLIOT: (*Glances around.*) I've only got *one* slut.

MRS ELLIOT: (*Ignoring him.*) I wonder how she'd like it? I wonder how she'd feel if I did go and see her family...and told them what she is? What she's *really*

like? A dirty little slut who hangs around the clubs...
after the old men...the married men...the worn-out
whoremasters! Because she can't get a man of her own! I
wonder what her family would say?

MR ELLIOT: They'd say: 'Oh.'

MRS ELLIOT: Eh?

MR ELLIOT: OH!

MRS ELLIOT: (*Raging.*) YOU'LL SEE!

MR ELLIOT: (*Goading.*) Don't forget about the office...

MRS ELLIOT: You're so cocky...

MR ELLIOT: Weren't you going to phone her boss and
give him a character reference too?

MRS ELLIOT: You'll see!

MR ELLIOT: I'll see what?

MRS ELLIOT: You'll see...

MR ELLIOT: So will you...
(*Silence. MR ELLIOT stares at her.*)
You know why I threatened to sell the house. I don't *wish*
to do so. I know the kids like it here...they've got plenty
of friends in the road...and the school's convenient...and
I know you like it...the neighbours...

MRS ELLIOT: (*Sobs.*) Pitied!

MR ELLIOT: (*Stunned.*) Eh?

MRS ELLIOT: Pitied by all of them!

MR ELLIOT: Eh? Pitied? BALLS! You like to imagine
you're an object of pity. It makes you feel noble.
(*Mounting frustration.*) You like to think you're the talk of
the wash-house... (*Old woman's voice.*) 'That poor,
benighted girl...so cruelly forsaken...a martyr to her
husband's lusts...bravely devoting her life to her two
lovely little children, struggling to give them a decent
upbringing...but oh! abandoned and alone...while her
swine of a husband squanders the family income on the
services of sluts and the company of drunkards!'

MRS ELLIOT: (*Laughs.*) That sounds a fair description.

MR ELLIOT: (*Carried away; raging.*) Hypocrites! I know
how they look at me when I come down the road. 'Look
out,' they whisper. 'Here comes Mr Elliot, the black

sheep of Greengate Avenue. Bring in the children and bolt the doors!' And the truth of the matter is…is that half the men are practising quiet, civilized adultery and the other half are aching for it…but without any nasty messy wounding things like *relationships*…and half the women would be only too happy if the men had a quiet, civilized thrombosis tonight! As long as there was no social stigma and the insurance was up to date.

MRS ELLIOT: Does that make you feel better? (*Silence. MRS ELLIOT turns to face him.*)

MR ELLIOT: (*Jaunty.*) Well…at least I'm honest about it!

MRS ELLIOT: What do you want? A medal?

MR ELLIOT: A word of recognition will do…or just a quiet ovation.

MRS ELLIOT: You are a bastard!

MR ELLIOT: I'm an honest bastard.

MRS ELLIOT: (*Contemptuous.*) Honest! You go on about honesty as if it meant a general amnesty. (*Pause. Then mocking.*) 'I destroyed my children, but I'm honest about it…' If every criminal was honest, it wouldn't reduce the crime rate!
(*Silence.*)

MR ELLIOT: (*Measured.*) I am not 'destroying the children'. I might have destroyed them had I stayed with you.

MRS ELLIOT: Huh!

MR ELLIOT: I'm not going to say that I left you purely 'for the sake of the children'.

MRS ELLIOT: No…you're not!

MR ELLIOT: …but they certainly suffer less from the separation than they did from the union!

MRS ELLIOT: Because they see less of you…

MR ELLIOT: Because they see less of…us. (*Opens the door, listens, closes it.*) You miss that, don't you? (*Bitter.*) You enjoyed those…performances. (*Compere's voice.*) 'THE VIRTUOUS MRS ELLIOT EXPOSES THE WICKED MR ELLIOT TO THE INNOCENT LITTLE ELLIOTS.'

MRS ELLIOT: *They had a right to know.*

MR ELLIOT: (*Emphatic.*) They had a right *not* to know!
(*Pause; turning away.*) Christ...we're off again. (*Recites.*)
You say alpha, I say beta, you say gamma, I say
delta...the dance of the dead language. (*Pause; now
recovering.*) You know...I think that was the worst thing
about those performances. We exposed the innocent little
Elliots to such a storm of obsolete phrases. Oh, we went
at it with a will...with whoops and war cries...a home-
made Western, with rusty guns and rubber arrows. (*Pause;
a bit sadly.*) It was poor stuff... (*More cheerfully.*) Well...at
least...they'll pass any examination on the more obvious
miseries of marriage, won't they?
(*MRS ELLIOT has not been listening to this speech. Silence.
Her foot jerks. MR ELLIOT stares at her.*)
(*Pleading.*) I want the children to have a chance. And I
want us to have a chance...you...me...but we have no
chance, none of us, while you and I are together. We've
tried it...it didn't work. All I'm trying to do...is to work
out a way of life that I can live...live honestly...without
going bent, or collecting little boys or something. Why
won't *you* try? Why?
(*MRS ELLIOT sits staring. MR ELLIOT moves to the
window, looks out at the garden. Turns and glances at the
kitchen, then looks critically round the lounge.*)
(*Harsh.*) What are you trying to do? Hound me with
guilt? (*Pause.*) Pressurize me back here? You won't!
(*He moves back and stands in front of MRS ELLIOT, who
ignores him.*)
I know your tactics. This act. This 'sloth pitch'. (*Pause;
then venomous.*) You're *willing* the weeds to grow and the
spiders to spin and the trays to rust...aren't you? (*He puts
his hands on the chair, leaning over MRS ELLIOT. His voice
is ugly with anger.*)
You can sit and stare till Doomsday but you won't
STARE ME BACK!
(*Silence.*)
MRS ELLIOT: (*Grimly.*) Are you living with that slut?
MR ELLIOT: (*Stunned.*) Eh?

MRS ELLIOT: You are…aren't you?

MR ELLIOT: (*Evasive.*) What?

MRS ELLIOT: (*Snaps.*) Has *she* got a washing machine…

MR ELLIOT: (*Thrown.*) Eh? *You've* got a washing machine…

MRS ELLIOT: …that doesn't work!

MR ELLIOT: (*Recovery – deadpan. Pause.*) Actually we live in a penthouse with a colour television suspended from the ceiling and eat…only at the best restaurants. (*Pause; then aggressive.*) Why did you ring me?

MRS ELLIOT: Huh.

MR ELLIOT: (*Sits down.*) I refuse to be trapped.

MRS ELLIOT: You trapped yourself.

MR ELLIOT: You set the trap.

MRS ELLIOT: You trapped both of us!

MR ELLIOT: And freed both of us.

MRS ELLIOT: You're not FREE!

MR ELLIOT: No? (*Pause; sings, romantic croon.*) 'I'll never be free-eeeee, from you and me-eeee…' (*Pause; then bitterly.*) Christ…I'm beginning to believe it too!

MRS ELLIOT: (*Satisfied.*) It's true.

MR ELLIOT: (*Explodes.*) BALLS!
(*Silence. MR ELLIOT walks to the window muttering 'Alphabetagammadeltaalpha' and back. Faces MRS ELLIOT.*)
(*Bitter but measured.*) Why are you so determined to get me back here? (*Pause.*) Why? (*Then with a touch of desperation.*) Are you still in love with me or what?

MRS ELLIOT: (*Flinches.*) Huh…

MR ELLIOT: (*Insistent.*) Or…do you just want your pound of flesh?

MRS ELLIOT: (*Stubborn.*) I want what I'm entitled to.

MR ELLIOT: What's that?
(*Silence. MRS ELLIOT stares ahead. MR ELLIOT stands facing her.*)
And what's that?

MRS ELLIOT: You know what that is…

MR ELLIOT: I don't. I don't know.

MRS ELLIOT: Oh…don't you?

MR ELLIOT: No…I don't know. (*Silence.*) You mean you're entitled to keep me in misery for the rest of my life?

MRS ELLIOT: (*Snaps.*) YES!

MR ELLIOT: You're doing that anyway. (*Pause.*) But you're not entitled to do it.

MRS ELLIOT: I am.

MR ELLIOT: You're not.

MRS ELLIOT: I am.

MR ELLIOT: You are not!

MRS ELLIOT: I am!

MR ELLIOT: (*Grim patience.*) *How* are you entitled to do it?

MRS ELLIOT: By the law.

MR ELLIOT: What law?

MRS ELLIOT: *The* law.

MR ELLIOT: That is not the law.

MRS ELLIOT: It *is* the law.

(*Pause.*)

MR ELLIOT: That is *not* the law! (*Pause.*) What law is that? The law says that you can marry and you can separate and you can, in certain circumstances, dissolve the marriage. You are not entitled to hound me! (*Pause.*) What law?

MRS ELLIOT: (*Shouts.*) The MORAL law!

MR ELLIOT: (*Stubborn.*) What moral law?

MRS ELLIOT: The moral law.

MR ELLIOT: You won't make it any clearer by parrotting it out. The moral law…the moral law…what moral law?

MRS ELLIOT: (*Very confident.*) There's only one moral law.

MR ELLIOT: You mean the law of the Jews two thousand years ago? (*Pause.*) They had their tablets – we have ours! (*Laughs.*) Every country has its own moral laws and they differ at different times. What would you be saying now if you lived in… (*Searching for a word.*) …Outer Polynesia? (*Pause – then heated.*) You know what I think is immoral? To perpetuate a destructive marriage. And it's especially immoral to do it 'for the sake of the children'. Because then you also perpetuate a destructive cycle that they will inherit.

MRS ELLIOT: Why don't you go and live in Outer Polynesia?

MR ELLIOT: I want the system changed!

MRS ELLIOT: You want people changed.

MR ELLIOT: (*Scornfully.*) Go on...tell me... 'People are the same everywhere'. They certainly manage to conceal their similarities! Maybe all of us...maybe we all want to feed and sleep and shag and crap...but we certainly devise different ways of organizing the process. (*Pause; then bitterly.*) And here...here in this little corner of the human nest...we've devised our own brand of organizing the mating and breeding process... West European Monogamy, *perpetua dormienda*! But the trouble is, the women are breaking out of the nest. They want more. They don't want to be stuck in the nest forever. (*Silence.*) Christ...only in the last century men could *sell* their wives in the market place...and there are quite a few who'd do it today given the opportunity! But it's all changing...people are changing...and the system has got to change too.

(*Pause.*)

Because women are growing up. The old-fashioned Mammie – like you – won't put up with Big Daddy's casual shags down the Dock Road or after the office party...she won't turn a blind eye like Grannie did. She blows up and issues ultimatums. When she says 'You're mine', she really means it.

While the new-fashioned Mammie, with her job and her car and her see-through bra, she wants a bit of what's going, for herself. *Her* credo is: If you shag, I shag. So the poor old male gets hammered either way...and he just can't stand it.

And marriage...as we've known it...marriage can't stand it either. I don't know whether we're going to develop some concept of 'Serial Marriage', where everyone *expects* to have a series of partners...Hollywood-style. Or whether we're just going to develop a new-style relationship that's permanent as long as it lasts...but with a hell of a lot more honesty from the beginning.

But one thing is certain...in future, men and women are going to share free and equal unions that last because they want them to last. Not because they're forced! And not because anybody *owns* anybody. Nobody can own anybody! (*Pause; then almost fervently.*) Free men...will live freely...with free women!

MRS ELLIOT: And who's going to bring up the children?

MR ELLIOT: Professionals.

MRS ELLIOT: Professional what?

MR ELLIOT: Pedagogues. People who freely choose to look after children.

MRS ELLIOT: You mean...you'd put the children in a home?

MR ELLIOT: (*Explodes.*) I'd put all the children of the world in a home! To learn to love. And I'd put all the adults of the world *in the world.* To learn to live. (*Pause.*) Oh, I know there'd always be a few frightened savages who'd prefer to stay down in the family pits...but the majority would jump at the chance of freedom.

(*Pause. MRS ELLIOT stares at the window. MR ELLIOT stares at her.*)

(*Intones like a butler.*) You rang? (*Silence.*)

Why did you ring me up?

MRS ELLIOT: Did we disturb you?

MR ELLIOT: What was the matter?

MRS ELLIOT: (*Mimicking.*) What was the matter?

MR ELLIOT: I dashed up here.

MRS ELLIOT: Ahhh...did you? (*Silence.*) I was going to kill myself...and the children.

(*Silence.*)

MR ELLIOT: Were you?

MRS ELLIOT: So I poured three glasses of Nembutal...to 'end it all'.

MR ELLIOT: You should have poured one for me too.

MRS ELLIOT: You're welcome...

MR ELLIOT: And why did you ring me? Did you want me to stop you...or just to watch?

MRS ELLIOT: I just thought you'd like to know.

(*MR ELLIOT goes to the table and examines the glasses.*)

MR ELLIOT: Is this it?

MRS ELLIOT: Drink it and see.

(*He picks up a glass. Looks at it. Puts it down.*)

MR ELLIOT: Well, as I always say...suicide's the one thing you never regret. (*Pause.*) You haven't had any of this already, by any chance?

MRS ELLIOT: Huh.

MR ELLIOT: You haven't, have you? (*Pause.*) And the kids...they're all right, aren't they?

MRS ELLIOT: You saw them.

MR ELLIOT: Are they?

MRS ELLIOT: Yes.

MR ELLIOT: I can't have you despatching all my problems at once, you know.

(*Long pause. MRS ELLIOT sits still. MR ELLIOT looks at her, then goes to the window and looks out. It is getting darker now. After a while he goes into the garden and collects the bicycle. He comes back in with it.*)

Have you got a rag?

(*MRS ELLIOT fetches a rag from the kitchen.*)

Don't want this going rusty.

(*He dries off the bicycle.*)

These brakes need tightening up... (*He works on the brakes.*) What did this cost? About thirty quid...wasn't it? (*Chuckles.*) Christ...I remember my first bike. A sit up and beg. My mam got it from a dump in Scotland Road...for fifteen bob...a real old wreck, but it went. (*Pause.*) Actually that old bike went for four years...then I sold it for nine bob. (*Pause; works on brakes, tests them.*) Then the old man took me into town for my fifteenth birthday and bought me a new Raleigh Sports...on the never-never, of course... I think that was the first H.P. form he signed in his life and he never really recovered. (*Laughs.*) It had low-slung handlebars...real racy...I painted it red and white. I had that bike for years and years...went everywhere on it.

MRS ELLIOT: You left it at the flat.

MR ELLIOT: Eh?

MRS ELLIOT: Don't you remember? You left it at the first flat we had. You were always going to go back and get it, but...don't you remember?

MR ELLIOT: Oh…yes…well, no, actually. I've got a lousy memory…it's self-deleting. (*Pause.*) My greatest gift! (*Silence.*)

MRS ELLIOT: I walked past that place last week.

MR ELLIOT: Which?

MRS ELLIOT: The house…they had a new fence round the garden…about six feet high…you couldn't see in.

MR ELLIOT: Oh…

MRS ELLIOT: Remember the old fence and the time it crashed into the street?

(*Pause. MR ELLIOT busies himself with the bike.*)

You had to take a day off work trying to get it back up.

MR ELLIOT: (*Uncomfortable.*) Yeah… (*Pause.*) Does Tony let Sarah ride this?

MRS ELLIOT: He would…but I won't.

MR ELLIOT: It's big for her, yet.

MRS ELLIOT: She tries to ride it in the garden. (*Smiles.*) If she had her way she'd be off down the motorway with it!

MR ELLIOT: Huh!

MRS ELLIOT: She's headstrong. (*Pause.*) She's got your… confidence.

MR ELLIOT: You know what she said to me on Sunday? She said: 'I *might* get married when I grow up…but I'm not going to marry a drunkard like you.'

MRS ELLIOT: Hmmm.

MR ELLIOT: (*Now nervously fiddling with the bike.*) This needs a drop of oil.

(*MRS ELLIOT fetches oil from the kitchen and watches him.*)

MRS ELLIOT: Sarah's a bit deceptive, though. She's got bags of confidence outwardly…in company…but underneath she's nervous…very impressionable. (*Pause.*) Tony's just the opposite. He won't open his mouth in company – he's a real gooseberry! People pat him on the head and tell him not to be shy and you can see him wilting on the spot. But all the time…underneath…he's really very sure of himself. In fact…he's probably *too* sure. He's arrogant.

(*MR ELLIOT finishes with the bike and puts it in the hallway.*)

MR ELLIOT: That should be okay.

(*MR ELLIOT comes back in and stands uncertainly. He goes to the sideboard and picks up a letter.*)

MRS ELLIOT: I think it's the gas bill.

MR ELLIOT: (*Opening it.*) Four pounds eighteen…that's not bad.

MRS ELLIOT: We haven't used much…with the warm weather.

MR ELLIOT: Did the man come about the telly?

MRS ELLIOT: No…I waited in, but there was no sign of him.

MR ELLIOT: Can you get a picture?

MRS ELLIOT: Just about.

MR ELLIOT: I'll give him a tinkle tomorrow.

MRS ELLIOT: I'm not bothered really…but the children like to watch.

MR ELLIOT: Yeah…I'll ring him tomorrow. What day?

MRS ELLIOT: What?

MR ELLIOT: What day shall I ask him to come?

MRS ELLIOT: Any day. I'm in every day.

MR ELLIOT: (*Uncomfortable.*) Yeah…well, I'll ask him to come as soon as possible.

(*Silence.*)

MRS ELLIOT: Did you see the photograph?

MR ELLIOT: (*Looking.*) Oh…when was that taken?

MRS ELLIOT: Last week…at school.

MR ELLIOT: Look at Sarah saying 'Cheese'. (*Laughs.*) Tony looks distinctly mutinous.

MRS ELLIOT: He hates having his photograph taken.

(*MRS ELLIOT gets up.*) I'll make a cup of coffee.

MR ELLIOT: Oh…thanks.

MRS ELLIOT: (*Going.*) There's a couple of snapshots there too.

MR ELLIOT: (*Looking at them.*) They're not bad, are they?

MRS ELLIOT: (*From kitchen.*) They were only a shilling each. (*Pause. MR ELLIOT stares at the three glasses.*)

MR ELLIOT: What about the big one?

MRS ELLIOT: That was twelve and six.

MR ELLIOT: I'll give you the money.

MRS ELLIOT: Oh...thanks.

(*MR ELLIOT looks at the photographs as MRS ELLIOT comes in with the coffee, puts it on the floor, and sits on the couch. MR ELLIOT glances slightly nervously at her as she sits, then looks back at the snapshots. MRS ELLIOT sits back, much more relaxed now.*)

MR ELLIOT: (*Almost shy.*) Can I have one?

MRS ELLIOT: One is for you.

MR ELLIOT: (*Awkwardly.*) Oh...right. (*Pause.*) Thanks. (*Pause.*) They look great. (*Long pause.*) I feel very proud of them.

MRS ELLIOT: Hm.

(*Silence. MR ELLIOT sighs heavily.*)

Still sighing?

MR ELLIOT: Eh?

MRS ELLIOT: You never stop sighing these days.

MR ELLIOT: It's a plea for sympathy...

MRS ELLIOT: Huh...

(*Silence. MR ELLIOT stares absently. MRS ELLIOT looks at him from the side.*)

You're beginning to spread...

MR ELLIOT: I drink too much.

MRS ELLIOT: So what's new?

MR ELLIOT: (*Glum.*) Now I drink too much too much.

MRS ELLIOT: (*Sympathetic.*) It's the Irish in you.

MR ELLIOT: No...as the old man used to say...it's just genuine undiluted greed.

(*Silence.*)

MRS ELLIOT: Why don't you go and see him?

MR ELLIOT: (*Flat.*) I couldn't face him.

MRS ELLIOT: (*Almost teasing.*) That's not like you!

MR ELLIOT: I don't want to hurt him...

MRS ELLIOT: It's amazing how you can care so much about 'not hurting' people...yet you strew your casualties all over the place!

MR ELLIOT: What casualties?

MRS ELLIOT: Your father, now. Your mother…once. Your children. Your…women. (*Pause.*) I know I'm not the first to suffer…and I won't be the last. (*Pause.*) It's not much of a consolation, but it's a help.
(*Silence.*)

MR ELLIOT: (*Meaning it.*) I *do* hate to hurt people.

MRS ELLIOT: I know. I know you do. But you can't keep your hands off people. You want to *save* them…

MR ELLIOT: Save them?

MRS ELLIOT: You're a real old Catholic missionary at heart. (*Laughs.*) Maybe you should have gone to Outer Polynesia!
You're drawn to people…like me, once…who are lonely, or shy, or…in some way, incomplete…and you can't rest until you…*complete* them. You offer them *your* vitality, *your* resilience, *your* confidence…but instead of saving anybody, you're actually enslaving them. (*Pause.*) It's funny to hear you going on about not 'owning' people, because in fact you insist on owning any woman you're in love with…that's your price…you have to *own* her – heart and mind and body, and past and present and future too! You…infiltrate…every particle. (*Pause.*) I feel sorry for you because I think you're innocent. (*Pause.*) But that's why you're so dangerous…because when you've satisfied your missionary zeal…when you've got your new convert, now dedicated, completely committed to you…what happens then? (*Pause.*) You drop her! BUMP! Down to earth again. And off you go galloping on your next crusade! (*Pause. MR ELLIOT turns to her.*)

MR ELLIOT: All this…because I walked out on you?

MRS ELLIOT: It's not just me.

MR ELLIOT: You're the one who matters…to you.

MRS ELLIOT: What about the first one?

MR ELLIOT: (*Slightly edgy.*) What first what?

MRS ELLIOT: (*Now also edgy.*) *Your* first one. (*Pause.*) The one that you used to go on about.

MR ELLIOT: (*Laughs.*) My *first* permanent relationship? She dropped me.

MRS ELLIOT: Huh! After you drove her to it! (*Silence. MRS ELLIOT stares intensely at him from the side.*) You know damn well that you would have dropped her if she hadn't dropped you! But that...that was just what you wanted her to do. You wanted the feeling of being betrayed, abandoned, et cetera, et cetera, et cetera...all the things you accused me of enjoying...because you revelled in the drama!
(*Silence.*)
What happened afterwards? When she came back... wanting to talk to you? She was desperate...but did you help her? (*Laughs.*) HUH! You wouldn't even talk to her. You hid in the lavatory! A grown man hiding in the lavatory from a girl who wants to talk! What a hero!
(*MR ELLIOT flinches. Stares straight ahead. MRS ELLIOT laughs sourly.*)
But I wasn't so obliging, was I? I wouldn't leave you. You had to leave me. *You* had to be the...'betrayer'. And you don't like that role nearly as much, do you? Your old Catholic conscience gives you hell, doesn't it?
(*Pause; then acidly.*) That's if you still feel *anything.*

MR ELLIOT: As you ask...

MRS ELLIOT: I didn't!

MR ELLIOT: ...As you evidently feel some curiosity about my spiritual condition, it might help you to know that I have enough anguish, guilt and remorse swilling about inside me to float a bloody monastery!

MRS ELLIOT: You should have gone on the stage.

MR ELLIOT: (*Ignores her.*) And if, to that brew, I add about ten pints of bitter ale, I can just about lurch from one derelict sunset to another. (*Laughs – bravado tone.*) I'm an apostolic alcoholic!
(*Long pause. MR ELLIOT is slumped back in the chair. The sun is now low in the sky. MRS ELLIOT glances at him. He rouses himself suddenly. His tone is weary and self-disgusted.*)
Christ...I'm tired of them!

MRS ELLIOT: (*Cautious.*) What?

MR ELLIOT: All my...untethered agonies. (*Pause; then in a firm, common-sense tone.*) Can't we be practical?

(*MRS ELLIOT does not reply or look at him.*)

We've been separated for three years. The law – the *law* – allows us to divorce by mutual consent after two years. (*Then nervously.*) We could do that now. (*Silence.*) But it also allows unilateral divorce after five years. So that I can divorce you, without your consent, in two years from now. (*Pause.*) Which I *will*. (*Pause.*) Why the hell not face up to it now, start again, get a job… (*Then pleading.*) You know I'll look after you and the kids… (*Now forceful.*) So why not be adult about the situation and –

MRS ELLIOT: (*Snaps.*) What about her?

MR ELLIOT: Who?

MRS ELLIOT: YOUR SLUT!

(*Pause. MR ELLIOT looks grim but ignores her.*)

How long is that going to last?

MR ELLIOT: It's a permanent relationship.

MRS ELLIOT: Huh! The only permanent relationships you have are with the past!

MR ELLIOT: She's my last and only love.

MRS ELLIOT: Huh…

MR ELLIOT: You think I'm beyond redemption?

MRS ELLIOT: Beyond repair. (*Pause.*)

MR ELLIOT: (*Then with some exasperation.*) Look…what are *you* suggesting we do? Are you suggesting we play the social game? So I live here…on a loose rein…and I'm allowed out every Friday night for some wild revel in the woods, after which I return – exhausted and seed-freed – to the old barred cell? Balls! I'm through with all that.

(*Pause. MR ELLIOT walks to the window. Very restless. His tone is urgent now, sincere.*)

Look…there's no need for…despair! Okay, you may wonder about the neighbours…but it's a nine-day wonder with them and they're probably consumed with envy in any case. (*Pause.*) They don't matter. (*Pause.*) And the children…I have a better relationship with them than I ever had. I used to curse their existence but now I…I'm proud of them, I'm happy with them…I love them, for Christ's sake!

MRS ELLIOT: (*Harsh.*) Because they're older...

MR ELLIOT: (*Snaps.*) Not just because they're *older...* because... (*Pause.*)

MRS ELLIOT: What?

MR ELLIOT: (*Determined.*) I'm happier with them because I'm happier without them.

MRS ELLIOT: Hmmm.

(*Pause. MR ELLIOT turns to face her. She moves to the chair facing the window.*)

MR ELLIOT: I wish it was simpler... You're an attractive woman...a good, selfless mother...and a jealous, vindictive wife. I wish you were just a one-hundred-percent bitch. It'd be a hell of a lot easier!

MRS ELLIOT: (*Sarcastic.*) I'm sorry...

MR ELLIOT: (*Very serious.*) Can I tell you something you won't believe?

(*Silence.*)

I have no wish to hurt you. (*She looks at him sourly.*) I don't want to damage you! I know your quality...and I don't want to humiliate you, to cheat you, to exploit you...to emotionally destroy you. That's why I left you! (*Silence.*)

MRS ELLIOT: (*Withering.*) Thanks.

MR ELLIOT: (*Dispirited.*) Ahhh.

MRS ELLIOT: (*Cynical.*) Still the old saviour? (*Laughs.*) Listen, the truth is, you do exactly what you want to do and you don't give a bugger who you destroy in the process. So...so carry on, do what you want to do, but just don't ask for my blessing.

MR ELLIOT: And what about you? Aren't you trying to force me to do what *you* want me to do?

MRS ELLIOT: Only the things you undertook – vowed – to do!

MR ELLIOT: Oh – not again!

MRS ELLIOT: So you did.

MR ELLIOT: So I did...subject to satisfaction.

MRS ELLIOT: You can't have marriage on free approval.

MR ELLIOT: (*Heated.*) And when a marriage breaks down – there's no law that would tolerate this sort of emotional blackmail! (*Points to the glasses.*) This...there's no law, moral or otherwise, that entitles you to threaten that you will kill yourself and murder the children...just so that you can 'have your way' with your errant husband.

MRS ELLIOT: My knight-errant husband.

MR ELLIOT: (*Raging.*) It's just blackmail!

MRS ELLIOT: (*Deadly pleasant.*) You know...you've given me an idea. If you really want to help...

(*Pause. MR ELLIOT looks at her.*)

It would be easier...and tidier...and we know how you care about tidiness...if *you* took the deadly draught, wouldn't it? Not here, of course...not in this room... (*Light laugh.*) You wouldn't want any corpses littering the lounge and frightening the children, would you? But somewhere... I know! In your penthouse! What about that? In your penthouse! Suicide seems more appropriate to a penthouse anyway, doesn't it? (*Very brightly.*) And I tell you what...maybe *she* would take a sip too...from the same glass! Yes...maybe you could *share the same glass* of nembutal, with different straws, of course...and sink simultaneously down together...like you always wanted! Then the children and I...would live happily ever after. How about that?

(*Silence. MR ELLIOT gives several slow handclaps.*)

MR ELLIOT: (*Urbane, philosophic tone.*) Yes, it's true... Marriage is one of the few surviving forms of ritual slaughter.

MRS ELLIOT: Oh well... (*Brightly.*) You're going to change everything, aren't you? You're going to change the system?

MR ELLIOT: (*Amused.*) Yes...I think I shall switch my efforts to saving society.

MRS ELLIOT: You're going to shatter the system...

MR ELLIOT: (*Smug.*) Yes.

MRS ELLIOT: ...which still satisfies the vast majority

MR ELLIOT: I'm a social catalyst.

MRS ELLIOT: (*Withering.*) A social misfit.

MR ELLIOT: Omega.

MRS ELLIOT: What?

MR ELLIOT: The language of love.

MRS ELLIOT: *You're* the linguist!

MR ELLIOT: (*Childlike recitation.*)

'Love that's loved from day to day

Loves itself into decay...'

MRS ELLIOT: Remember that...for future reference.

(*Pause.*)

MR ELLIOT: No...we should never have married.

MRS ELLIOT: (*Brittle.*) *We* should never have met.

MR ELLIOT: (*Theatrical.*) WE should never have been born!

MRS ELLIOT: (*Vicious.*) Somebody should have *told* your mother.

(*MR ELLIOT goes to slap her, but stops.*)

MR ELLIOT: You slut...

MRS ELLIOT: You buck...

MR ELLIOT: I'm going.

(*MR ELLIOT moves to go...looks at the glasses...hesitates.*)

MRS ELLIOT: Go on then... (*Shouts.*) GO!

(*MR ELLIOT puts on his coat.*)

MR ELLIOT: Are you going to be sensible?

MRS ELLIOT: (*Harsh.*) Are you going to grow up?

MR ELLIOT: (*A plea.*) You'll have to come to terms with it.

MRS ELLIOT: I have done.

MR ELLIOT: (*Surprised.*) What?

MRS ELLIOT: (*Confident.*) My terms.

MR ELLIOT: What do you mean?

MRS ELLIOT: I've come to *my* terms.

MR ELLIOT: I don't accept *your* terms.

MRS ELLIOT: You will.

(*Silence. MR ELLIOT turns decisively and moves to the door.*)

MR ELLIOT: I'll see you on Sunday...usual time.

MRS ELLIOT: If you go through that door...I'll kill myself and the children.

(*Silence. MR ELLIOT turns at the door and stares at her. Long pause. He tugs at his coat.*)

MR ELLIOT: I'll see you on Sunday...at two-fifteen...as usual. (*He goes.*)

(*MRS ELLIOT stares after him. Then she gets up, goes to the glasses. She looks at them. She takes hold of one. Pause. She takes all three in her hands and takes them to the kitchen. She hurls them into the sink.*
She returns, stops, looks at door, listens. Pause. Then she sits. Her foot jerks. She ignores it and remains staring straight ahead.)

Curtain.

THE SEA ANCHOR

Characters

LES
twenties

ANDY
thirties

SYLVIA
teens

JEAN
twenties

The action takes place during a day and the following morning in a jetty in Dublin Bay.

Across the stage runs a promenade with a vividly painted frontage of hotels, boarding houses and souvenir shops. Along the sea edge of the promenade runs a railing to which lifebelts are strapped. From the centre of the promenade a huge ramp thrusts forward and down into the auditorium. The ramp is made of timber and is supported by rusty iron piers. It is ancient and scarred by years of wear and exposure.

The Sea Anchor was first performed at the The Theatre Upstairs at the Royal Court Theatre in July 1974, with the following cast:

LES, Peter Armitage

ANDY, David Daker

SYLVIA, Alison Steadman

JEAN, Marjorie Yates

Director Jonathan Hales

Designer Sue Plummer

Lights John Tindale

ACT ONE

Afternoon, bright sunshine. ANDY sits on the ramp and scans the sea through binoculars. LES walks along the promenade, stops at the top, scans the sea, takes a bottle from his pocket and drinks. Both men wear shirts and jeans; ANDY wears an anorak and LES the jacket of an old suit. LES carries a newspaper.

LES: No sign yet?

ANDY: Eh?

LES: No sign of him yet?

ANDY: No.

LES: Fucking hero.

(LES spits in the water. Comes down the ramp.)

ANDY: There's the ferry...going back to Liverpool.

LES: It's the Liverpool ferry.

ANDY: *(Waves.)* All the best! Good luck!

LES: They'll need it.

ANDY: Tomorrow we'll be on it.

LES: Never mind...we've got all day.

ANDY: *(Leers.)* And all night, dear...

LES: I'll drink to that. *(LES drinks.)*

ANDY: I'll join you.

(ANDY takes a long drink. LES watches.)

LES: You wanna go easy with that. *(LES squats by ANDY, opens the paper.)* There's a big gang of reporters waiting for him at the hotel. Look at this... *(Reads.)* 'THE SOLO SAILOR. Nick Anderson, thirty-one-year-old father of four, sets off on solo sail from Liverpool to Dublin in a ten foot dinghy. Nick told our reporter that the voyage was his personal response to the challenge of the New Elizabethan Age.' *(LES hoots.)*

ANDY: So he got his picture in the paper.

LES: Gloryhound. *(Pause. LES looks through the binoculars.)* He's late isn't he?

ANDY: He said about eighteen hours...

LES: I thought by now we'd be doing the town.

ANDY: Yeah.

(*ANDY takes another drink.*)

LES: By the time he arrives you're gonna be legless.

ANDY: I'm legless now.

LES: Yeah...you had a load on the ferry.

ANDY: It's a tradition. Every year, Nick and me...we get pissed on the ferry coming over, pissed in Dublin, and pissed on the ferry going back.

LES: And then have a drink in Liverpool.

ANDY: To round off the weekend.

LES: Baffles me why we bothered to bring the girls.

ANDY: I warned you.

LES: What?

ANDY: I told you not to bring Sylvie.

LES: I'd never have heard the last of it.

ANDY: Why?

LES: Once Nick invited Jean I had to invite Sylvia.

ANDY: The two of you...you're too soft with women. What's the point of bringing your mistress on a dirty weekend? It's worse than bringing your wife. (*Silence.*)

LES: Have you got anything lined up?

ANDY: A beauty.

LES: Who?

ANDY: Fat Annie.

LES: She sounds a beauty.

ANDY: She's shaped like a tent. Lovely. She could sleep six of us. You should have seen her last year with Nick and me. She was insatiable.

LES: Both of you?

ANDY: What a woman. (*Pause.*) Nick's the only man I know who can down six pints and come six times in the one night. But Annie...

LES: Wish I'd been there.

ANDY: I'll introduce you tonight.

LES: No point –

ANDY: You'll like her.

LES: I'm stuck with Sylvia.

ANDY: Pity. (*Silence.*)

LES: It is a pity.

ANDY: You could have had a go at Annie.

LES: Very kind.

ANDY: (*Genteel.*) Oh, don't mention it.

LES: I meant kind of her. (*Pause.*) Pity, that. I just fancy a bit
of strange, too.

ANDY: I had a bit of strange last night.

LES: Did you?

ANDY: Yeah, I fucked the wife. (*Pause.*) Whenever I'm off
on a dirty weekend I make sure I fuck the wife before I
go, and she shuts up.

LES: I fuck mine when I get back.

ANDY: You should never neglect your marital obligations.

LES: No.

ANDY: After all a wife is a human being.

LES: Yes.

ANDY: She needs a fuck as much as we do.

LES: That's true.

ANDY: What else is there? A feed, a fuck, a good kip...

LES: (*Arch.*) Have you ever been in love?

ANDY: In love? Once...when I was young and green. Never
again.

LES: Why not?

ANDY: It interfered with the fucking. All this sex talk is
making me thirsty.

LES: Let's go and grab a pint.

ANDY: No...we better stay here. He's due now.

LES: He's overdue.

ANDY: Yeah...

LES: We're not gonna stay here, are we? All day?

ANDY: Let's hang on for a bit longer.

LES: Hey, Andy...

ANDY: Yes, Lesley?

LES: Have you got any Durex?

ANDY: Never use them. I prefer it in the raw.

LES: Catch a dose.

ANDY: I've fucked over 300 women, never caught a dose.
Had a spot of NSU once.

LES: NSU?

ANDY: Pissed hot needles for a week. But never had a dose.

LES: I wouldn't risk it without a contraceptive.

ANDY: I never use them. It's like picking your nose with your gloves on.

LES: You must leave a trail of bastards behind you.

ANDY: I never stay around to find out. (*Pause.*)

LES: I wonder if I can get any here?

ANDY: (*Mock shock.*) They wouldn't allow such filth in Ireland! You'll just have to pull out. What's Sylvia like on the job?

LES: Avid.

ANDY: Oh…avid.

LES: When we're on the job she snorts and trumps.

ANDY: The dirty bitch! Hey…would she make a foursome up with Annie?

LES: (*Looks up the ramp.*) Ask her.

(*JEAN and SYLVIA come down the ramp.*)

ANDY: Hey, Sylvie…

SYLVIA: What?

ANDY: Will you do me a favour?

SYLVIA: What is it?

ANDY: (*Leers.*) Nothing, really…

SYLVIA: (*Giggles.*) Oh, anything for you, Andy.

ANDY: (*Seizes her.*) Really?

SYLVIA: Sod off!

ANDY: (*Nuzzling.*) Flesh!

SYLVIA: Les…help!

ANDY: In five minutes you could make me a happy man.

SYLVIA: Leggo, you're pinching.

ANDY: Are you still wearing that pink corset? I've told you it's too tight.

SYLVIA: What's the favour?

ANDY: I want you and Les to join me and my lady friend tonight.

SYLVIA: What? For a drink?

ANDY: And for some fun and games…

SYLVIA: You can sod off.

ANDY: There…what did I say? When a woman's in love she loses all sense of adventure.

SYLVIA: I'm quite satisfied with Les.

ANDY: But is he satisfied with you?

SYLVIA: I think so.

ANDY: Note of hesitation there.

JEAN: No news yet? (*Pause.*)

ANDY: No.

JEAN: He's very late, isn't he?

ANDY: You getting impatient?

JEAN: No, but –

LES: Maybe we oughta go and check with the coastguard.

ANDY: Could do…

SYLVIA: The hotel bar was packed with reporters.

LES: Did you get a free drink?

SYLVIA: We got two actually. They were very hospitable,
    weren't they, Jean?

ANDY: It's an Irish tradition.

LES: Would they be as hospitable to Andy and me?

JEAN: They were just after a story.

ANDY: Which we shall give them! A story of heroism…

LES: You can tell he's had a few.

ANDY: You wouldn't understand it.

LES: What?

ANDY: The challenge of the ocean.

LES: It's not an ocean, it's a sea.

ANDY: It's an alien element.

LES: What?

ANDY: It's alien. Makes you feel puny…yet big.
    (*LES smiles at the girls and chuckles.*)
    Would you have the guts to tackle that crossing?

LES: No chance.

ANDY: Then you can't talk. (*Pause.*) Thank God there are
    some real men left.

LES: Huh!

ANDY: It's our tradition…the English heritage…the island
    race…

LES: The armchair Vikings.

ANDY: It's in our blood. Listen, in the last century an
    Englishman sailed to the Baltic in a converted lifeboat.

Now thousands of people… Look, when I was a kid you never even saw a car in our street in Liverpool. Now you see not just cars but boats as well…and at the weekends they'll all off to the Lake District, or the Welsh coast…thousands of them, messing about in boats.

LES: It's an excuse for escaping from the wife and kids.

ANDY: You know Nick and me were planning to buy one?

SYLVIA: (*Impressed.*) Buy a boat?

ANDY: We've been paying out a fortune in hire charges so we thought we'd buy one between us. Have some fun then…

SYLVIA: Great!

LES: What kind of boat?

ANDY: We'd like an ocean racer for nine grand but we'll probably get a second-hand dinghy for twenty quid.

LES: Roll on.

ANDY: (*Leering.*) Very handy for the weekend.

LES: (*Sings.*) 'On the good ship Venus
    My God you should have seen us…'

ANDY: Nice and compact.

LES: (*Sings.*) 'Wanking on the planking…'

SYLVIA: Oh Les!

LES: What?

SYLVIA: I think it sounds marvellous.

ANDY: Yes, we could have some nice weekends down in Holyhead.

SYLVIA: Could I come?

ANDY: There's a bench reserved for you.

LES: What's wrong with the back of the car?

SYLVIA: That's all I ever get from him.

LES: Haven't heard you complain.

SYLVIA: I hate making love in the back of a car.

LES: Try the front if you like.

SYLVIA: Is that all you want me for?

LES: What?

SYLVIA: You know what.

LES: What?

SYLVIA: Sex.

LES: I thought that was what you wanted me for?

SYLVIA: I think you are sex-obsessed.

LES: If you'd let me know how you felt I would've made alternative arrangements.

(*Silence. ANDY stands, scans the sea.*)

ANDY: No...you can't beat it. I remember one Saturday morning, cruising off Holyhead, a few weeks back. I got up very early, put the breakfast on...Nick was still snoring. I came out and had my first piss of the day. I remember standing there...there wasn't a soul in sight...just a tiny twist of smoke on the horizon...and all I could hear was the waves sucking the hull...fibreglass hull...the cry of a seabird...and the bacon sizzling on the old Primus! I stood there, stretched out my arms, filled the old lungs with ozone, and I thought: 'This is the life.'

LES: Here we go again.

ANDY: The sea is different from the land.

LES: Yes, it's the water.

ANDY: Don't you feel it?

LES: What?

ANDY: (*Arch.*) The lure of the deep.

LES: The lure of my arse.

ANDY: Don't you feel the romance of sailing?

SYLVIA: He hasn't an ounce of romance in him.

ANDY: Don't you?

LES: You know what cured me of the romance of sailing?

ANDY: What?

LES: Three years in the Merchant Marine.

ANDY: That's not sailing. That's like working in a floating factory. Might just as well be on land. Now in a pocket cruiser or a dinghy –

SYLVIA: Hey, could we go for a sail?

LES: We're going for a sail.

SYLVIA: When?

LES: Tomorrow, on the ferry.

SYLVIA: I mean in a boat. A little boat. Could we?

LES: You go.

SYLVIA: Will you?

LES: No.

SYLVIA: Why not?

LES: I don't want to.

SYLVIA: Oh, please Les...I'd love to go for a sail.

LES: I don't like sailing.

SYLVIA: Why not?

LES: The sea can drown you.

ANDY: Where's your spirit of adventure, man?

LES: (*Points between his legs.*) Here.

    (*SYLVIA slaps LES lightly.*)

SYLVIA: Cheeky bugger! Nick didn't have much experience of sailing, but look at him, sailing the Irish Sea...

LES: That proves he's a real man.

SYLVIA: Yes.

LES: (*Tough guy tones.*) Well, either you've got it or you haven't, I guess. (*Pause.*) I tell you one thing. I'd rather be sitting here than sitting out there. (*Laughs.*) Huh...

ANDY: Whatever you say about Nick, he's a man. He does exactly what he wants to do. He's a real man. (*Pause.*) I never really thought he'd do it.

SYLVIA: What made him do it?

ANDY: It was just a...a sudden decision. We were talking about our weekend here...you know, planning the trip on the ferry...

JEAN: Planning the orgy?

ANDY: We never *plan* our orgies.

JEAN: Don't you?

ANDY: We just create conditions that are conducive to them.

JEAN: Huh...conducive.

ANDY: Anyway, I happened to mention these students that were gonna sail from Blackpool to the Isle of Man on a mattress. (*Laughs.*) On a mattress! I thought they were nuts... But Nick was very impressed. The next thing I knew he was buying sailing magazines and talking like an old salt. Spent a fortune on charts and almanacs.

(*Silence. LES takes a drink from the bottle. Passes it to SYLVIA, who drinks. She offers it to JEAN, who refuses. Passes it to ANDY, who drinks.*)

LES: Maybe we ought to organise shifts?

JEAN Could he have gone in another part of the harbour?

ANDY: No, he'd come in here. Easier to lie up here. (*Pause.*) Anyway…if he came in the coastguards would let us know.

JEAN: I think we ought to go and ask them.

ANDY: Ask them what?

JEAN: About Nick. (*Silence.*)

SYLVIA: Where are we going tonight?

ANDY: Everywhere!

SYLVIA: Are there as many pubs as people say?

ANDY: Oh aye, it's a very civilised city.

SYLVIA: I can't wait…

ANDY: We'll go to Mooney's, you'll like that.

SYLVIA: Has it got a juke box?

ANDY: It's full of dockers and coalmen.

SYLVIA: Thanks very much!

ANDY: What's wrong with dockers and coalmen?

SYLVIA: Is there anywhere we can have a dance?

ANDY: (*Mock shock.*) Dance?

SYLVIA: I'd enjoy a dance. Wouldn't you, Jean?

ANDY: Sylvia darling…we're not going out to enjoy ourselves, we're going out boozing. If you want entertainment we'll go to Searson's.

SYLVIA: Do they have a show?

ANDY: Yes…you can always count on a good punch-up.

SYLVIA: Huh…

(*SYLVIA grimaces. Takes a swig from the bottle and passes it to LES. He drinks then tosses the bottle into the water.*)

LES: That's killed that.

ANDY: Nick'll pass it on the way in.

LES: I shoulda stuck a message in to say we'd be in the ale house.

ANDY: He's missed the tide.

LES: Yeah…

(*SYLVIA scans the sea through the binoculars.*)

SYLVIA: It's nice and clear.

(*She offers the binoculars to JEAN.*)

JEAN: No...once I start looking I'll never stop. (*SYLVIA looks up and follows the flight of a bird.*)

SYLVIA: Oh, look at this bird.

ANDY: Beautiful.

SYLVIA: Wish I could fly.

LES: You lot should have been birds and fishes. (*Silence.*)

ANDY: It's nearly half-four.

LES: Yeah...

ANDY: You think we should go and have a talk to the coastguards?

LES: Might as well.

ANDY: See what they say...

LES: Be here all day otherwise. And all night.
(*ANDY and LES stand.*)

JEAN: I'll come with you.

ANDY: No, you stay here.

JEAN: I wanna hear what they say.

ANDY: He'll probably come sailing in soon as we go.

JEAN: Oh...all right. Will you come straight back?

ANDY: Promise. We'll only be a few minutes.

SYLVIA: No diversions, now.

LES: What?

SYLVIA: If you're going to the alehouse I'm coming with you.

LES: We'd never dream of going to the pub without you.

SYLVIA: Hmmm.

ANDY: And we'll bring a bottle back with us.

JEAN: Huh!

ANDY: Relax...talk about us while we're gone.
(*ANDY and LES go off. SYLVIA sits.*)

SYLVIA: (*Jumps.*) Jesus! That's hot...feels as if it's gonna burst into flame. (*Wriggles.*) Your knickers stick to your arse.
(*Pause. SYLVIA examines the woodwork, brushes it, examines her dress, brushes that.*)
Do you think this dress looks all right?

JEAN: Very sexy.

SYLVIA: (*Giggles.*) That's what Les said.

JEAN: Does he like it?

SYLVIA: Oh, he can't stand it.

JEAN: Why?

SYLVIA: He'd have me wearing a boiler suit all the time.

JEAN: Is he very jealous?

SYLVIA: He's mad. Mind you...I'm jealous myself.

JEAN: Are you?

SYLVIA: Aren't you?

JEAN: I can be.

SYLVIA: You're bound to be jealous if you're really in love.
  (*Pause.*) Do you feel jealous of Nick's wife?

JEAN: No.

SYLVIA: Don't you?

JEAN: You wanna see her.

SYLVIA: What's she like?

JEAN: Fat.

SYLVIA: Is she? Mind you...she's had four kids, hasn't she?

JEAN: She's still fat.

SYLVIA: Yeah. I'd hate to be fat. (*Pause.*) Mind you, I'd like
  to have kids, wouldn't you?

JEAN: No thanks!

SYLVIA: Wouldn't you?

JEAN: No.

SYLVIA: I don't mean I want them now...but, you know,
  later.

JEAN: Later?

SYLVIA: When I'm older. I think kids give you something
  to live for when you're older.

JEAN: I've got something to live for already.

SYLVIA: What?

JEAN: Me.
  (*SYLVIA giggles. Silence.*)

SYLVIA: Would your husband like kids?

JEAN: Oh, he would...

SYLVIA: Would he?

JEAN: Yes, to tie me down.

SYLVIA: What did you tell him about the weekend?

JEAN: Said I was gonna spend it with my mate in
  Nottingham.

SYLVIA: Does he mind?

JEAN: He doesn't have any choice.

SYLVIA: Does he believe you?

JEAN: He'd swallow anything.

SYLVIA: And have you really got a mate in Nottingham?

JEAN: Yes. She wouldn't let me down. She couldn't afford to.

SYLVIA: Eh?

JEAN: She uses me as an excuse whenever she wants a dirty weekend.

SYLVIA: That's awful, that...

JEAN: What?

SYLVIA: The way people say 'dirty weekend'. You go away with someone you love and they call it a 'dirty weekend'! Huh...it sounds like me mother. (*Pause.*) I could do with an arrangement like yours...with your mate.

JEAN: I don't know...it's too easy.

SYLVIA: What?

JEAN: Sometimes I wish I could just tell my husband the truth.

SYLVIA: Tell him the truth!

JEAN: Yes.

SYLVIA: Why?

JEAN: It'd be simpler.

SYLVIA: What would he do?

JEAN: I don't know. Collapse, I suppose.

SYLVIA: Would he?

JEAN: Yeah.

(*Both women laugh.*)

SYLVIA: Does he have anyone else?

JEAN: How do you mean?

SYLVIA: I mean...does he have any affairs?

JEAN: I wish he would.

SYLVIA: Do you? Really?

JEAN: Yes, I do. But he lives for me.

SYLVIA: (*Smiles.*) Does he?

JEAN: Stupid bastard.

SYLVIA: Oh, Jean!

JEAN: He's like a big baby. If I say 'Boo' to him he goes off into a mood...won't eat, can't sleep and has a headache all week. See what you're missing?

SYLVIA: Missing?

JEAN: You're free.

SYLVIA: Who...me?

JEAN Yes...you can do what you like.

SYLVIA: You haven't met my mother.

JEAN: What's she like?

SYLVIA: Oh, she's a terror. She's still living in the nineteenth century. You know...

JEAN: Yes.

SYLVIA: She hasn't got a clue about what goes on in the world.

JEAN: Does she know about Les?

SYLVIA: You must he joking! A married man? She'd throw me out.

JEAN: Would she?

SYLVIA: I had to spin a yarn to get away for the weekend.

JEAN: What did you say?

SYLVIA: Said I was gonna see an old mate of mine in London.

JEAN: Who's the mate?

SYLVIA: That's the trouble.

JEAN: What?

SYLVIA: I haven't got one. (*They laugh.*) If only you could be honest about it...

JEAN: When you think of all the effort we put into planning and plotting...

SYLVIA: Yeah...

JEAN: All of us...the men and all...

SYLVIA: I know...

JEAN: If we put it into a business we'd all be millionaires.

SYLVIA: We would and all. (*Pause.*) But what else can we do?

JEAN: Sometimes I feel like just going down to Lime Street and getting the first train out and just...vanishing.

SYLVIA: Sometimes I feel the same.

JEAN: Why don't you get a flat?

SYLVIA: That's what Les says.

JEAN: Why don't you?

SYLVIA: He said once that if I got a flat then he'd leave home and join me.

JEAN: He said that?

SYLVIA: Yes. When he was drunk. (*Silence.*) Anyway...they all say that, don't they?

JEAN: Who?

SYLVIA: Married men.

JEAN: Nick never said it to me.

SYLVIA: I'm just so uncertain...

JEAN: You mean about Les?

SYLVIA: What?

JEAN: You mean about the way you feel for Les?

SYLVIA: Oh no. No...I've always been certain about that, ever since we first met.

JEAN: Have you?

SYLVIA: Yes.

(*Silence. JEAN studies SYLVIA.*)

JEAN: What's the problem then?

SYLVIA: It's just...making the first move, like. (*Pause.*) Les left home once before, you know.

JEAN: Did he?

SYLVIA: Yes.

JEAN: Did he get a flat?

SYLVIA: He went to live with some girl in Manchester.

JEAN: What happened?

SYLVIA: He said he got sacked from his job and had to go back home. And his wife was hysterical and there were the kids...and...

JEAN: Yes.

SYLVIA: So...I don't know.

JEAN: God, these wives. (*Silence.*)

SYLVIA: Are you hoping to get together with Nick?

JEAN: I don't know.

SYLVIA: You've been going with him for ages, haven't you?

JEAN: Five years.

SYLVIA: But aren't you miserable, just...just...

JEAN: 'Drifting'?

SYLVIA: Yes.

JEAN: If you can drift along in marriage you can drift along in adultery.

SYLVIA: I hate that word!

JEAN: What?

SYLVIA: 'Adultery.'

JEAN: Huh…that's the word. (*Laughs.*) Anyway, as Nick always says, it's only adultery after sunset.

SYLVIA: What?

JEAN: In the eyes of the law.

SYLVIA: It sounds so ugly.

JEAN: Well, that's the word.

SYLVIA: I mean, you have a serious relationship with Nick. You've known each other five years. Les and me…we've only known each other six weeks.

JEAN: That's your strength.

SYLVIA: What?

JEAN: Your strength is that you've only known each other six weeks. My weakness is that we've known each other five years.

(*Silence.*)

SYLVIA: But isn't there any hope you'll ever get together?

JEAN: Nick lives in hope.

SYLVIA: Would he leave his family?

JEAN: He hopes they'll get run over or die suddenly in their sleep.

SYLVIA: Oh…

JEAN: I don't know whether I'd want him to leave them.

SYLVIA: Don't you?

JEAN: I don't know how that would work out. (*Pause.*) Things are pretty cushy for me at home. I've got my husband, and he's…all right. He never interferes and he's always there. Whereas with Nick…huh!

SYLVIA: What –

JEAN: I wouldn't want to take the place of his wife. I wouldn't put up with it.

SYLVIA: But if you and he were together…

JEAN: What?

SYLVIA: Wouldn't that be different?

JEAN: Yes…then he'd be trampling over me instead of her.

SYLVIA: Oh…

JEAN: Nick isn't the one-woman type.

SYLVIA: Isn't he?

JEAN: No. (*Silence.*) He's been unfaithful.

SYLVIA: When?

JEAN: When?

SYLVIA: When has he been unfaithful?

JEAN: A few times.

SYLVIA: I mean…in the morning, or…

JEAN: (*Laughs.*) Or after sunset? I don't think the hour of the day affects me. (*Pause.*)

SYLVIA: No, no. Oh well…it's always the same with a married man, isn't it?

JEAN: And what about Les?

SYLVIA: What?

JEAN: How do you feel about Les?

SYLVIA: I've never felt about anyone the way I feel about Les.

JEAN: What, never?

SYLVIA: No.

JEAN: Your first love?

SYLVIA: Yes. Don't you believe me?

JEAN: I believe you. And how does Les feel?

SYLVIA: He says I'm the first woman he's ever *really* loved.

JEAN: Congratulations. (*Silence.*)

SYLVIA: You don't like him, do you?

JEAN: Who…Les?

SYLVIA: Yes.

JEAN: He's not really my type.

SYLVIA: What do you mean?

JEAN: He's too hard.

SYLVIA: Les isn't hard!

JEAN: Isn't he?

SYLVIA: I know he acts hard, but…but that is only an act.

JEAN: Is it?

SYLVIA: We all do that, don't we? (*Silence. SYLVIA glances around at the promenade, then more quietly.*) I'm dreading telling him I've started.

JEAN: You've started?

SYLVIA: Yes. My period.

JEAN: I would've thought he'd have been relieved?

SYLVIA: He'll say I've ruined the weekend. (*Pause.*) Jean…

JEAN: What?

SYLVIA: I don't suppose you've got any towels?

JEAN: Towels?

SYLVIA: I didn't expect to start till next week, but I suppose with all the excitement…anyway I was caught without any sanitary towels. I've had to use cotton wool.

JEAN: You still use towels, do you?

SYLVIA: Yes.

JEAN: I always use Tampax, I might have one at the hotel…

SYLVIA: I can't use them.

JEAN: (*Laughs.*) Oh, Sylvia! Everyone can.

SYLVIA: I've tried. I can't get it in.

JEAN: Why?

SYLVIA: I'm too tight.

JEAN: You're not putting it in properly. Let's see if I've got any at the hotel, and if I have I'll show you how to put it in.

SYLVIA: Will you?

JEAN: Yes.

SYLVIA: I hope you have.

JEAN: We must be able to get some anyway. After all, even the Irish have periods!

(*SYLVIA sees the men on the promenade.*)

SYLVIA: Shhhh.

(*Silence. ANDY comes down the ramp followed by LES.*)

ANDY: They've called an alert.

JEAN: An alert?

SYLVIA: Oh God!

ANDY: Don't panic…

SYLVIA: I hope he's all right.

ANDY: They would have waited a bit longer but they've had a flash from the Met Office. There's some dirty weather on the way.

JEAN: What do they do?

ANDY: They alert vessels in the sea area. And they send out the helicopters to do a pattern search, and the lifeboats...

SYLVIA: I hope they find him...

ANDY: He's in a busy channel, and it'll be light for a while yet.

SYLVIA: Thank God for that.

ANDY: They should spot him pretty quickly.

JEAN: What did they say?

ANDY: What?

JEAN: What did they think could have happened?

ANDY: He might have had a spot of engine trouble...the outboard might have packed in for some reason. Or he might just have gone off course. (*Pause.*) They contacted the English coastguard.

JEAN: The English?

ANDY: Yes...in case he'd gone back.

JEAN: He'd never have gone back.

ANDY: They had no news of him. (*Silence.*)

SYLVIA: What'll we do?

LES: Let's all go and have a drink somewhere.

ANDY: We'd better be at the hotel...just in case...

LES: We could let them know where we're going.

ANDY: I've gotta go back to the hotel anyway, to ring his wife.

JEAN: Nick's wife?

ANDY: She rang earlier...left a message at the hotel.

JEAN: What message?

ANDY: She just asked if Nick would ring her when he came in. I better let her know...

JEAN: The bitch couldn't wait.

(*JEAN walks up the ramp.*)

SYLVIA: Jean...are you going back to the hotel?

(*JEAN goes off without answering.*)

Oh God...

LES: What?

SYLVIA: I wonder what's happened to him?

LES: Either he's afloat, in which case he'll turn up sooner or later. Or he's not, in which case he won't.

SYLVIA: Don't say that.

LES: Nothing we can do.

(*SYLVIA starts up the ramp. LES takes her arm but she shrugs him off.*)

Where are you going?

SYLVIA: The hotel.

LES: Let's go and have a drink somewhere.

SYLVIA: I'm going back to the hotel.

LES: What for?

SYLVIA: Jean's gonna get me some Tampax. (*SYLVIA goes off.*)

LES: I hope it chokes you.

ANDY: I better go and ring his wife.

LES: What are you gonna say?

ANDY: Make a date for next week. (*Pause.*) Jean's a right little cow, isn't she?

LES: She's a match for Nick.

ANDY: Huh... She's worse than his wife. She's been driving Nick nuts lately, you know.

LES: Has she?

ANDY: His wife turns a blind eye to his whoring around but Jean...Jesus!

LES: Like having a second wife.

ANDY: Yeah. Well...I better go and ring her. (*Grimaces.*) Oh, I hate talking to that woman. She'll be hysterical...

LES: Then we can go and inspect a few alehouses, eh?

ANDY: What about Jean?

LES: What about her?

ANDY: Hadn't we better stay with her?

LES: She won't thank you for it.

(*ANDY starts up the ramp.*)

What about your girl friend?

ANDY: Who?

LES: Annie.

ANDY: (*Smiles.*) Oh... Fat Annie?

LES: You gonna ring her?

ANDY: I don't know…

LES: Tell her about me.

ANDY: Why? You game?

LES: Always game.

ANDY: I don't know…

LES: Why don't we go and see her now?

ANDY: I think I better stay with Jean. You coming?

(*LES watches him go, then turns and looks seawards.*)

LES: Bang goes me night in Dublin!

(*LES picks up the newspaper and looks at the picture of Nick in the boat. Tears up the paper and throws it into the sea.*)

Blackout.

ACT TWO

Late night. A yellow fog. The ramp dimly illuminated by the lamps on the promenade JEAN sits huddled in a coat and scarf. Distant foghorns. ANDY comes along the promenade. Peers down the ramp, then comes down to JEAN.

ANDY: You'll catch your death. (*ANDY sits.*) Be a bit more comfortable in the hotel. (*Silence.*) I was up at the Coastguards. Hell of a job in this weather. The fog... (*ANDY takes out a bottle, offers it to JEAN, who ignores it. He drinks.*)
They're still out there...still searching. Hell of a job. (*Pause.*) The reporters have gone home. Les went into town for a drink with Sylvie. The hotel's dead. (*ANDY studies JEAN. Silence. Then he hugs her.*)
Don't worry...

JEAN: Huh.

ANDY: If he doesn't make it, you can sleep with me.

JEAN: Thanks.

ANDY: Does he know I'm the other man?
(*Silence.*)

JEAN: What did his wife say?

ANDY: What?

JEAN: You rang her, didn't you?

ANDY: Aye, I rang her.

JEAN: What did she have to say?

ANDY: She asked me to give you her regards and said to remember you're always one of the family.

JEAN: What was her reaction?

ANDY: Hysterical.

JEAN: Huh...

ANDY: Whenever I speak to that woman she seems to be in the state of, or on the verge of the state of, hysteria.

JEAN: What *did* she say?

ANDY: You want to know? (*Pause.*) She said Nick was a child who'd been led astray by bad companions.

JEAN: That'd be the day...

ANDY: What?

JEAN: Nick led astray…

ANDY: And she said that she was sick of him tomcatting around and making a fool of himself with some little slut.

JEAN: Huh! What did you say?

ANDY: (*Pompous.*) I agreed.

JEAN: Of course.

ANDY: I agreed with every word she said.

JEAN: You would.

ANDY: My wife was standing next to her. (*Pause.*)

JEAN: Is she a friend of your wife's?

ANDY: Not exactly a friend –

JEAN: What?

ANDY: More of an ally. (*Laughs.*) Yes, his missus and mine, they're old allies. The two of them are waiting up tonight in our house.

JEAN: I bet she's revelling in every minute of it.

ANDY: It's a rare chance.

JEAN: Was that all she said?

ANDY: Apart from a few shrieks and moans. Oh and she said she didn't know what was gonna become of her and the kids, because Nick hasn't paid the insurance for over six months.

JEAN: That sounds like her. (*Silence.*) I wonder what he's doing now…

ANDY: I bet he's dying for a pint.

JEAN: I bet he's wishing he'd come with us on the ferry.

ANDY: He's probably drifting.

JEAN: Drifting?

ANDY: Yeah…he'll know they're looking for him by now. (*Silence.*)

JEAN: I can't imagine it…out there…

ANDY: It's not so bad.

JEAN: Isn't it?

ANDY: It's fascinating.

JEAN: In that fog?

ANDY: I remember one time a few weeks back Nick and me were caught in a fog. We'd been practising a spot of celestial navigation –

JEAN: What?

ANDY: Celestial navigation…sailing by the stars. We ran into a real pea-souper. Couldn't see a thing. And then after a while it lightened and the visibility was about fifty yards. The light was yellow and the sea was all black and placid. It was strange…eerie. And then we heard this hissing sound and we saw this thing like a wave coming at us…not really a wave, though, more like a giant ripple…

JEAN: A ripple?

ANDY: Yeah…a giant ripple, V-shaped, about five yards across and seven yards fore and aft…and it came hissing along just by the boat.

JEAN: What was it?

ANDY: We didn't have a clue…till it passed by. And then Nick said: 'It's mackerel. It's a shoal of mackerel!' And they were so close you could have dipped your hand in and picked a few up.

JEAN: What happened?

ANDY: This great 'V' went hissing off into the sea.

JEAN: Weird. (*Silence.*) What time is it?

ANDY: Near midnight.

(*ANDY offers the bottle to JEAN, who shakes her head. ANDY drinks.*)

Fancy Les going off into town.

JEAN: He would. (*Silence.*)

ANDY: I hadn't realised how bad things were between Nick and his wife.

JEAN: What?

ANDY: She said that he came in about four o'clock in the morning one night last week –

JEAN: What night?

ANDY: She didn't say. Anyway, she made him something to eat…

JEAN: She waits up for him.

ANDY: Yeah, anyway, she asked him where he'd been and he stuck the breadknife through the coffee table. (*Pause.*) So…she screamed at him and he stood up and spat in her face.

JEAN: Oh...lately he's been...he's been going berserk.

ANDY: I know he's been throwing it back.

JEAN: Eh?

ANDY: The booze.

JEAN: Oh yes...he drinks all day, and he's never at work and he's deep in debt...he's in debt up to his neck, you know...and he worries, and then he drinks even more...

ANDY: If he didn't drink he might shoot himself.

JEAN: Or he might get some work done.

ANDY: I don't know...

JEAN: And he's playing around more than ever. Anything in a skirt...

(*Silence.*)

ANDY: His wife asked me to have a talk with him.

JEAN: A talk?

ANDY: Yeah, she said...she asked if I'd have a talk with him. A fatherly talk. Give him some sensible advice, like. Tell him to mend his ways before it's too late.

JEAN: She must have a lot of faith in your influence.

ANDY: She has.

JEAN: And in you...

ANDY: She knows me as a quiet religious man devoted to his family and his dog.

JEAN: Does your wife believe that?

ANDY: She prefers to believe that. Though I don't know...I am like that...by and large.

JEAN: I offered to do something for Nick that his wife would never do.

ANDY: What?

JEAN: Leave him.

ANDY: Leave him?

JEAN: Yes...free him.

ANDY: What did he say?

JEAN: Said he didn't want to be free of me.

ANDY: I don't think he does.

JEAN: He acts like it.

ANDY: Yeah, but... (*Pause.*) It's tough for his wife, though, with four kids.

JEAN: Nobody forced her to have them. (*Silence.*)

ANDY: I think we all worry too much about these things. You know, we create drama –

JEAN: Do you think I ought to leave him?

ANDY: No. No, he depends on you.

JEAN: I left him for a week a few months back...but he started ringing every day, and meeting me outside the office, and in the end...inevitably...we got back together again. But the only time he pays me that kind of attention is when I do leave him. It's no basis for a relationship, is it?

ANDY: (*Breezy.*) We're all like that.

JEAN: I'm not.

ANDY: You're a woman.

JEAN: I wouldn't put up with it except that there's just no other man who's given me what he gives me. And I've had plenty... (*Pause.*) I can't imagine living without Nick. And every so often I could strangle him.

ANDY: That's natural. (*Silence.*) You know...out there, out at sea...it's strange. You feel as if you're the only thing living and yet all around, only feet away, are millions of life forms.

JEAN: (*Shivers.*) I'd find that very scary.

ANDY: I find it reassuring.

JEAN: Do you?

ANDY: (*Laughs.*) Depending on the forms of life.

JEAN: How do you mean?

ANDY: There was one time both of us were terrified. We saw a fin break surface near the boat, then another, then another. Fins popping up everywhere. I grabbed an oar and shouted to Nick, 'SHARKS!'. I thought we were gonna be eaten alive.

JEAN: I didn't know there were sharks off England.

ANDY: Oh, sometimes...anyway, we stood there gripping the oars and looking at these black bodies, big buggers, leaping up and down in the sea. It was night and the sea was silver and we could see them flashing up and down. And we could hear them barking...kind of a hoarse barking. And then Nick said: 'Jesus, they're playing!' Sharks don't *play*. And we realised they were a school of porpoises. Yeah, they were porpoises, big soft buggers, a big gang of them, dancing all round the boat, playing together.

JEAN: (*Laughing.*) Oh...

ANDY: We were so relieved we started laughing and shouting out to them. Our voices were booming in the fog, all hollow. And they took fright and shot away through the fog...still barking. I'll never forget them.

JEAN: That's something new to think about.

ANDY: What?

JEAN: Sharks.

ANDY: No...no, it's a million-to-one chance. At least, at sea, you know who your friends are and who your enemies.

JEAN: Why take such risks?

ANDY: Why not?

JEAN: I don't see the point.

ANDY: You can step off the side and get run over any day.

JEAN: Les was right, for once.

ANDY: What?

JEAN: He said you were as crazy as Nick.

ANDY: It was perfectly feasible. It was a perfectly feasible exercise. I admire him immensely for doing it.

JEAN: You would.

ANDY: You forget...men receive knighthoods for such...feats.

JEAN: (*Scoffing.*) Knighthoods...

ANDY: Yes.

JEAN: Men receive knighthoods for writing songs nowadays.

ANDY: That's different.

JEAN: Is it?

ANDY: Course it is! But when a man does something really heroic I think it's only right that it should be recognised. And I for one salute him. (*ANDY takes a swig from the bottle.*) Yes I do! (*ANDY salutes.*) I salute Nick and all men like him. Because they restore my faith in human nature. Because they're the real *men*...they do something with their lives while the rest of us sit on our backsides and –

JEAN: Did his wife really say that about me?

ANDY: What?

JEAN: The 'little slut'...

ANDY: She didn't name any names.

JEAN: Oh...

ANDY: No. She might have been talking about somebody else.

JEAN: I see.

(*SYLVIA comes along the promenade. ANDY hears her, turns.*)

ANDY: That you, Sylvie?

JEAN: Yes.

ANDY: Come and join the party.

(*SYLVIA steps down the ramp, unsteadily. ANDY helps her down.*)

Christ...I thought you were gonna dive in then. You had a skinful?

SYLVIA: Yeah...

ANDY: Where is he then?

SYLVIA: God, I'm freezing.

ANDY: Put this round you. (*ANDY offers his anorak.*)

SYLVIA: I'm all right.

ANDY: Put it on.

(*ANDY helps her into the anorak. They sit.*)

SYLVIA: What about you?

ANDY: What?

SYLVIA: You'll be cold.

ANDY: I'll cuddle up to you. (*ANDY hugs her.*)

SYLVIA: (*Smiles.*) Sod off.

ANDY: Where is he then?

SYLVIA: Who?

ANDY: Bluebeard.

SYLVIA: Oh, he's in the pub. I left him in the pub.

ANDY: (*Seizes her.*) Is there time for a quick one before he comes back?

SYLVIA: Lay off.

ANDY: Jean'll keep watch.

SYLVIA: Don't...

(*ANDY releases her and she sits slumped.*)

ANDY: What's the matter?

167

SYLVIA: I feel sick.

ANDY: You won't throw up on my anorak, will you?

SYLVIA: No…

ANDY: Is there anything the matter? (*Silence.*)

SYLVIA: No news?

ANDY: No.

(*SYLVIA whimpers.*)

Have a drop of this.

SYLVIA: I couldn't.

ANDY: You'll feel better.

SYLVIA: I couldn't take it.

ANDY: It'll warm you up.

SYLVIA: No…I've had too much to drink already.

ANDY: (*Mock moralising.*) See…there you are…serves you right…a young girl like you, out drinking with married men…

SYLVIA: He wouldn't come outa the pub.

ANDY: What pub?

SYLVIA: A pub in town.

ANDY: (*Laughs.*) Did you expect him to?

SYLVIA: I was feeling unwell. (*Sobs.*) It was horrible in there. All smoky and scruffy and all full of men.

ANDY: Sounds just like home.

SYLVIA: I was feeling dizzy and there was nowhere to sit. I had to hold onto the bar. And Les…Les said I was making a show of myself in front of the men. But when I asked him to go he wouldn't, he told me to… 'Fuck off.' So I hit him.

ANDY: (*Laughs.*) You hit Les?

SYLVIA: I slapped him and then I ran out.

JEAN: Good for you.

SYLVIA: All the men were laughing. (*Silence.*) All those men in there…

ANDY: What?

SYLVIA: They were all standing there with their pints in their hands looking at me as if they'd never seen a woman before.

ANDY: Over here they lead sheltered lives. (*Silence.*) You're trembling.

SYLVIA: I'll be all right.

ANDY: You'd better go to bed.

SYLVIA: I'm all right.

ANDY: Don't take any notice of Les.

SYLVIA: What?

ANDY: You know what he's like when he's had a few.

SYLVIA: It's too much...

ANDY: What?

SYLVIA: I'm browned off with it...

ANDY: What you need is a good kip.

SYLVIA: No...I'm sick of it...I'm sick of all of it...

ANDY: You'll feel better in the morning...

SYLVIA: I'm through with it all.

ANDY: Come on...I'll take you back to the hotel.

(*ANDY takes her arm, half rises. SYLVIA doesn't move.*)

SYLVIA: No...

ANDY: Come on.

SYLVIA: I wanna stay here.

ANDY: Why?

SYLVIA: I wanna stay here with you.

ANDY: Come on back. You won't miss anything.

SYLVIA: I'll be all right in a while.

(*Silence. ANDY sits back. Drinks. Offers the drink to the women. Neither takes it. After a moment a torch flashes on the promenade. LES comes on and walks to the top of the ramp. Holds the rail and peers down at the others. Flashes the torch at them. Then descends the ramp with great care. Flashes the torch at SYLVIA.*)

LES: Hello, darling.

SYLVIA: Sod off!

LES: Charming. (*Flashes the torch on the jacket.*) Are we all wearing each other's clothes now?

ANDY: She was cold.

LES: I'm bloody freezing. (*LES flashes the torch seawards.*) What's the plan then? (*Pause.*) See fuck all in this fog.

ANDY: Les...

LES: What?

ANDY: Sylvie's not well.

LES: No, she's pissed.

ANDY: Don't you think you ought to take her to bed?

LES: (*Drawls.*) What a topping idea!

    (*LES formally offers his arm to SYLVIA.*)

SYLVIA: Fuck off!

LES: Now she's quoting me!

ANDY: Come on, Sylvie…

    (*SYLVIA rises to join ANDY.*)

LES: Where are you going?

ANDY: I'll take her across to the hotel.

LES: You gonna put her to bed?

ANDY: I'll just take her across…

LES: I couldn't allow it.

ANDY: What?

LES: I couldn't let her go with you.

ANDY: Stop acting –

LES: Put my sweetheart in the clutches of a known lecher?
    I'd never forgive meself!

    (*LES bars the way. ANDY lets go of SYLVIA. She sits down.*)

ANDY: Les…

LES: What, darling?

ANDY: She ought to be in bed.

LES: I second that.

ANDY: Let her go…

LES: She won't come with me. (*LES flashes the torch at
    SYLVIA.*) She's gone off me…

ANDY: Lay off.

LES: (*To SYLVIA.*) You gonna stay here all night?

SYLVIA: Yes!

LES: Won't do any good staying here. (*Then hearty.*) I know!
    Why don't we all go into town and get pissed?

SYLVIA: Huh!

LES: Did you speak?

SYLVIA: You're pissed already.

LES: You can talk.

SYLVIA: He can hardly stand up.

LES: (*Injured.*) I'm just...just getting my second wind. (*LES flashes the torch seaward and peers through the binoculars.*) See fuck all here. Hardly see the water. It's like looking down the lavo. (*Silence.*) Never find him in this fog.

ANDY: Sit down, Les.

LES: In this fog...you wouldn't find a liner, never mind a frigging dinghy. So what about it, mate?

ANDY: What?

LES: You're the brains of the operation.

ANDY: What do you mean?

LES: What's the plan?

ANDY: We wait.

LES: What? All night?

ANDY: Till he makes it.

LES: If he makes it. Coulda been rammed by a bloody liner, nobody'd ever notice. (*Silence.*) Great night out, this. More like a bloody wake.

ANDY: I'll go up to the coastguards.

LES: Ahhhh...action!

SYLVIA: I'll come with you.

(*ANDY walks up the ramp. SYLVIA follows. LES joins her – walks by her side. SYLVIA stops. LES stops. SYLVIA starts up the ramp and LES accompanies her. SYLVIA stops.*)

LES: Shall we dance?

SYLVIA: Are you going or not?

LES: I was just gonna ask you that.

(*SYLVIA sits down.*)

You better give him his anorak back.

SYLVIA: What?

LES: Give him it back and you can have my jacket. (*LES starts taking off his jacket.*)

SYLVIA: (*Calls.*) Andy.

ANDY: (*From the promenade.*) What?

SYLVIA: You better take your anorak.

ANDY: Don't worry about it.

LES: There's a gentleman for you. (*LES examines the bottle then offers it round. Silence. He drinks.*) Nobody join me? You miserable bitches! Cheers! Hey... did you hear about the man with red hair? (*Pause.*) The body of a man with red hair was washed up on the Isle of Man.

JEAN: How did you hear that?

LES: Heard it on the radio.

JEAN: Well...Nick didn't have red hair.

SYLVIA: It was more of a light brown.

LES: It had golden glints in the sunlight. (*LES drains the bottle and throws it into the water.*)

JEAN: Did you mean that about the liner?

LES: What?

JEAN: Ramming the dinghy.

LES: Could happen.

JEAN: Anything *could* happen.

LES: It's a busy channel.

JEAN: But the chance of a collision...

LES: Wouldn't have to be a collision.

JEAN: What?

LES: Pass nearby would do it. Little boat like a dinghy, get swamped in the wake of a powerboat. Wouldn't have to touch. Nobody'd notice. (*LES goes to the side of the ramp.*) 'Scuse me, ladies...while I tap this kidney. (*He urinates.*)

SYLVIA: Don't listen to him...

JEAN: What?

SYLVIA: He's just trying to stir it up.

JEAN: Oh...

SYLVIA: I know...he's after blood.

JEAN: But what he said –

SYLVIA: He's exaggerating.

JEAN: Why?

SYLVIA: I told you – he's out for blood.

(*LES comes back.*)

LES: Ladies shouldn't whisper.

JEAN: Were you exaggerating?

LES: Did she say that? (*LES flashes the torch in SYLVIA's face, then JEAN's.*) You believe me don't you?

SYLVIA: Leave her alone.

JEAN: Oh, let him play.

LES: Never had so many laughs in me life! (*LES stands at the front of the ramp and flashes the torch out to sea: two short bursts, then one long, then one short.*)

SYLVIA: What's he doing now?

LES: Distress signal.

SYLVIA: What?

LES: (*Shouts.*) 'I AM DISABLED. COMMUNICATE WITH ME.'

JEAN: You'll have the coastguard in here next.
(*LES focuses awkwardly on his watch.*)

LES: Jesus! Near eleven!

SYLVIA: Why don't you go to bed?

LES: (*Coy.*) If you come with me...

SYLVIA: Bugger off.

LES: Didn't come all the way to Dublin to sleep on me own.
(*LES flashes the torch in a wide arc across the sea, slowly.*)
No sign. Nothing. Nobody there.
(*Silence. ANDY comes down the ramp.*)

ANDY: I bumped into one of the coastguards. They've called off the search.

SYLVIA: Oh God...

ANDY: Till the fog lifts. They say it's even worse out there. It's hopeless searching...and it's dangerous for the lifeboats.

JEAN: What about Nick?

ANDY: They've done all they can.

SYLVIA: What could have happened?

ANDY: If he had mechanical trouble then he's probably just riding it out.

JEAN: You mean drifting?

ANDY: I mean riding it out on the sea anchor. It's not a proper anchor...really only a kind of parachute you throw over the side and it fills with water and keeps you in place...holds you steady...well, pretty steady. (*Pause.*) They'll find him in the morning. (*Pause.*) They said they'd send a message across to the hotel if there's any... (*Pause.*) I suppose I better go and ring my missus...

JEAN: And his.

ANDY: What?

JEAN: Isn't his wife staying at your house tonight?

ANDY: Yeah, that's right.

JEAN: You'd better tell her the good news.

ANDY: Yeah…no point in them staying up all night for nothing. (*ANDY starts up the ramp, stops.*) Are you coming over?

JEAN: No.

ANDY: There's no point in staying here.

JEAN: Go and make your phone call.

ANDY: Sylvie…

SYLVIA: What?

ANDY: Don't you think you better get to bed?

LES: She wants to be here, in the reception committee. (*Silence. Stands.*) I don't know about you but I came over to see the inside of the pubs and that's what I'm gonna do. How about you, Andy? (*Pause.*) We can keep in touch with the hotel. Ring back every fifteen minutes.

ANDY: Yeah, we could.

LES: That's what Nick would do.

JEAN: If he'd had the radio…

LES: What?

JEAN: If only he'd the radio…

LES: He had a radio. I got him a radio.

JEAN: With flat batteries!

LES: He shoulda got new ones.

JEAN: You knew what would happen.

LES: I told him he was crazy.

JEAN: And then you got him the equipment…

LES: Christ, first I'm at fault for not getting the gear, and now I'm at fault for getting it.

JEAN: He couldn't have gone otherwise.

LES: Anyway Nick was supposed to get his own equipment. But I had to spend two whole days running round the town getting it for him. He spent the whole of last week in the alehouse talking about the trip – and getting free drinks on the strength of it.

JEAN: I didn't see you refusing any.

LES: What?

JEAN: You were there with him. You encouraged him to drink.

ANDY: Nick never needed much encouragement to drink.

JEAN: Oh, you were just as bad.

ANDY: Eh?

JEAN: Worse, in fact, because he trusted you. He thought you were his friend.

ANDY: What are you on about?

JEAN: You encouraged him to spend all his time in the pubs and in the clubs so he never got a stroke of work done...wasting his life. I think you wanted to see him go to pieces because you were jealous of him. And that's why you encouraged him in this...this madness...

SYLVIA: Jean, be fair!

JEAN: What?

SYLVIA: Everybody wanted to help Nick.

JEAN: Oh, you're all as bad, all of you.

SYLVIA: You can't blame them.

JEAN: It was you who encouraged him most of all.

SYLVIA: Me?

JEAN: You know...

SYLVIA: I didn't want him to sail.

JEAN: You know what I mean.

LES: What do you mean?

JEAN: (*Mocking.*) 'Oh Nick you're so brave...'

SYLVIA: I never said that.

JEAN: I can imagine.

SYLVIA: You never heard me say that.

JEAN: What did you say? (*Pause.*)

LES: What are you saying?

JEAN: Don't you know? (*Silence.*)

SYLVIA: Christ... You're both writing him off.

LES: (*To JEAN.*) What do you mean by saying she encouraged Nick?

SYLVIA: You're both talking as if he had no chance.

LES: Shut up. (*Then to JEAN.*) What do you mean?

JEAN: Ask her.

LES: You seem to know a lot about it.

JEAN: I got it from the source.

LES: What are you talking about? (*Then to SYLVIA.*) What's
    she talking about?
    (*SYLVIA jumps up to join ANDY.*)
SYLVIA: I don't know! I'm sick of both of you and your
    squabbling –
    (*LES holds her.*)
LES: Tell me what she means.
SYLVIA: Leave me alone!
LES: When you tell me.
SYLVIA: Ask her. Ask her. I don't know.
LES: Don't you?
SYLVIA: NO!
LES: I think you do.
SYLVIA: Let me go. I feel sick!
    (*LES releases her and she slides to the ramp. He stoops down
    by her.*)
LES: Sylvia…please…
SYLVIA: Leave me alone…
LES: I only wanted to know what she was –
    (*SYLVIA retches. LES turns and looks at JEAN.*)
    Satisfied?
JEAN: What?
    (*LES slaps JEAN and she falls back. LES stands, starts up
    the ramp.*)
LES: I'm going. I've had a bellyful of this –
JEAN: Nick had her in the back of the car last week on the
    beach at Freshfield. Didn't you hear? It was all round the
    alehouse.
    (*Silence. LES looks at JEAN. ANDY steps down the ramp.*)
ANDY: Jean.
JEAN: Wasn't it?
LES: Is that true?
ANDY: For Christ's sake, Jean!
JEAN: Ask him.
LES: (*To ANDY.*) Is that true?
    (*LES looks at ANDY. Silence. ANDY stoops to SYLVIA. LES
    bars his way.*)
ANDY: She's sick…
LES: Hang on.

ANDY: Let's get her to bed.

LES: Is that true?

ANDY: All this fuss about a fuck...

(*ANDY moves back from LES. LES stoops to SYLVIA.*)

LES: I knew there was something. I could sense it. All week I could sense something. And then I knew. When he was sailing off I knew. You shouted: 'Goodbye, lover!' Didn't you? 'Goodbye, lover!' That's what you shouted to him. Those were your last words to him. 'Goodbye, lover!'

(*LES touches SYLVIA's neck. She sobs.*)

Sylvia...

SYLVIA: What?

LES: (*Anguished.*) Why did you do it with him?

SYLVIA: I don't know what you want!

LES: What?

SYLVIA: I don't... (*Hysterical.*) I don't know what you want of me. You say you want me and you make love to me and you never...you never...

LES: What?

SYLVIA: ...give...

LES: Give?

SYLVIA: You never give me anything...

LES: Oh Christ!

SYLVIA: You never give me any hope...for...

LES: (*Hard.*) Why did you let him do it?

(*SYLVIA sobs. ANDY tries to get JEAN to go. She doesn't move. ANDY stands uncertainly.*)

SYLVIA: And you turn on me and swear at me and...mock me...and I don't...I don't know what you want of me. I don't know!

(*SYLVIA slumps down on the ramp. She retches. LES stands.*)

ANDY: Let's get her to bed, Les.

LES: No.

ANDY: We've gotta get her to bed.

LES: You do it.

ANDY: What?

LES: One thing I could never do...

ANDY: What?

LES: Fuck a woman that's drunk. (*LES goes up the ramp.*)

ANDY: Les…

LES: What?

ANDY: You can't leave her…

LES: Can't I?

ANDY: She's sick.

LES: Is she? So am I.

ANDY: She needs you…

LES: I'd rather stick it in a jar of worms. (*LES goes off.*)

ANDY: (*Stooping.*) Sylvie…

SYLVIA: I'm sorry…

ANDY: It's all right.

SYLVIA: Has he gone?

ANDY: Just lie still for a bit.

SYLVIA: (*Weeping.*) I didn't mean to…to…

ANDY: Shhhhh.

SYLVIA: Jean…

 (*JEAN looks at SYLVIA.*)

 I'm sorry…I was feeling so low…

ANDY: Don't worry about it.

SYLVIA: All I know is…I do love Les. I do. But he never gives me any hope! (*Sobbing.*) I know he won't forgive me but I do love him. He won't believe me but he's the one I love…the only one… He's the first man I ever loved and the only man I ever could love…

JEAN: Oh, belt up.

 (*Silence. SYLVIA pulls herself up. She takes off ANDY's anorak and lets it fall to the ramp. She goes up to the top of the promenade and looks left and right.*)

SYLVIA: (*Shouts.*) Les. Les!

 (*SYLVIA runs along the promenade and off. ANDY steps up the ramp as if to follow then stops. Turns and looks at JEAN. JEAN stares out to sea. Silence ANDY walks slowly up the ramp and off. JEAN sits rigid staring ahead. Yellow fog swirls around.*)

Lights fade.

Blackout.

ACT THREE

The next morning. A grey day with light rain. JEAN sits on the ramp. huddled in a raincoat. ANDY walks along the promenade. stops, looks out to sea for a moment. Comes down the ramp. Glances at JEAN, then looks through the binoculars.

ANDY: Thank God it's cleared up. (*Pause.*) Why don't you go and get some breakfast? They're still serving.

JEAN: I don't want any.

ANDY: (*Hearty.*) What...when it's paid for?

JEAN: Mine isn't.

ANDY: What?

JEAN: I haven't got any money to pay the bill.

ANDY: Oh, don't worry about that. I'll look after that. (*Silence.*) You ought to eat some breakfast. (*Pause.*) Seen anything of Les and Sylvia?

JEAN: No.

ANDY: They weren't at breakfast. (*Pause.*) I always say you should start the day with a good breakfast. (*Silence.*) When did they start the search?

JEAN: First thing this morning, when the fog lifted.

ANDY: I didn't wake up till nine o'clock.

JEAN: Have you rung home?

ANDY: Eh? Oh, yes. Yes I spoke to the missus. You wouldn't believe it, but...she stayed up all night. I mean, she's never had a good word to say for Nick, but she stayed up all through the night.

JEAN: With his wife?

ANDY: Aye.

JEAN: Did you go into Dublin?

ANDY: I'd arranged to meet someone. (*Silence.*) If I'd known you were gonna stay here all night...

JEAN: There wouldn't have been any point in you staying here.

ANDY: No, but...

JEAN: I'm sorry about last night.

ANDY: What?

JEAN: The things I said to you.

ANDY: Oh, forget it.

JEAN: I meant what I said to Les.

ANDY: It's best forgotten.

JEAN: No...I did mean it. (*Pause.*) Anyone can see he's got her on a string...

ANDY: He's a funny bloke.

JEAN: It just makes me mad to see the way he uses her. And she's so bloody naive...

ANDY: She's only in her teens.

JEAN: She'll be naive when she's ninety.

ANDY: She's innocent.

JEAN: She's not innocent, she's naive. (*Silence.*) Nick and I had a terrible row about her.

ANDY: Did you?

JEAN: Seems so stupid now. But...he said she threw herself at him. And I said if he had to jump into the back of the car with every little cow that came along, well...we might as well finish. (*Pause.*) It brought things to a head, I didn't *want* to finish, but I thought it might he better for him.

ANDY: Yeah...

JEAN: And he agreed...

ANDY: Did he?

JEAN: Then the next day he went down on his knees and begged me to start again.

ANDY: Huh...

JEAN: I just blew up.

ANDY: Did you?

JEAN: I told him...said he didn't know what the hell he wanted, or didn't want...me, or his wife, or a string of little cows, or...or all of it or none of it. And I asked him if he thought this...this pantomime was going to solve anything.

ANDY: What did he say?

JEAN: He said, 'No, but it'll be a laugh.'

ANDY: Sounds like Nick.

JEAN: It was just...bravado. (*Pause.*) I didn't care if
   he...screwed the odd scrubber now and again. It meant
   nothing to me. I could stand it if he could. But he
   couldn't... He let it go to his head.

ANDY: He's a romantic.

JEAN: What?

ANDY: I think what it was with Nick, he got married too
   early. He was only in his teens when he married. He
   never really had time to enjoy himself. And then in his
   thirties he realised he'd missed out. He felt cheated. But
   instead of being honest about it he convinced himself
   there was some real change in society. You know the way
   he used to rant on...he looked at the teenagers and
   convinced himself that they were free...sexually free, in
   a way we hadn't been. Rubbish! We were all at it when
   we were teenagers, just the same. Nothing's changed.
   Maybe a bit more open nowadays, but that's all. But
   Nick...he really swallowed all this rubbish you read in
   the magazines...

JEAN: I think his trouble was that he still thought it was an
   achievement if he slept with someone.
   (*LES comes down the ramp.*)

LES: No news...

ANDY: No. Thank God it's cleared –

LES: Bad.

ANDY: What?

LES: I would have thought they'd have spotted him by now.

ANDY: They've only had a couple of hours...give them
   time...
   (*Silence. LES sits.*)

JEAN: There was a man at the coastguards' stayed up all
   night trying to contact him on the radio...just in case he
   could receive a message.

ANDY: Nick might have received it then.

JEAN: Hmmmmm.

ANDY: He's got all he needs to last for a week.

JEAN: Except the batteries.

LES: Don't start on that!

JEAN: That was the most important thing.

ANDY: Everything's important when you're out there.

LES: Look...look at this.

> (*LES takes a list from his pocket and tries to show it to JEAN.*)
>
> (*Reads.*) Spare jerrycan of petrol
>
> First Aid box
>
> Binoculars
>
> Rope
>
> Magnetic compass
>
> Sea anchor
>
> Torch
>
> Alarm clock
>
> Christ, he's got all he needs and more! Look, safety harness, food hamper, brandy, thermos flask –

JEAN: And you didn't put any sugar in the coffee.

LES: I what?

JEAN: You didn't put any sugar in his coffee.

LES: Christ!

JEAN: Nick can't drink coffee with no sugar in.

LES: Then he'll die of thirst.

JEAN: You can laugh.

LES: If he dies of thirst I'll never forgive myself. (*Silence.*) If he'd allowed a bit more time for the preparations he could have had his sugar, and his batteries. But he was so bloody cocky – so eager to get away –

JEAN: Cocky?

LES: Yes, cocky...he talked as if he could wade across.

JEAN: He can't even swim.

LES: He can't swim?

JEAN: No.

LES: Jesus.

JEAN: He said it wouldn't make much difference anyway if...

LES: I suppose he might get a lift from a passing liner.
(*Silence.*)

JEAN: Even at the last minute he might have called it off if it hadn't been for you.

LES: Yeah, blame me.

JEAN: He said he wanted to call the trip off.

LES: When?

JEAN: When he was sitting in the dinghy…

LES: Oh yeah!

JEAN: I heard him say, 'Let's call it off.'

LES: He chickened out.

JEAN: He was worried about the engine.

LES: That was only an excuse.

JEAN: I heard him say it would never work.

LES: You think I was gonna let him get away with that after all I'd had to do? I fixed the sparking plugs, didn't I? And then he snapped the shearing pin on a rock when he was manoevring the dinghy to give the photographer a better shot. I had to go down into the water, dick first, to get to the propeller shaft. I got soaked to the waist while he was sitting there in his sailor cap chunnering away, 'Let's leave it, it'll never work!'

JEAN: And you pushed him off!

LES: Yes, I did. And I took great pleasure in doing it. I took three steps in the water and give the dinghy an almighty shove and shouted: 'FUCK OFF TO IRELAND!'
(*LES laughs sourly.*)

JEAN: I hope you're pleased now.

LES: Look… Nick would never have cancelled his trip with all the reporters there and all the pricks from the Yachting Club standing around laughing at him. He'd left it too late by then. You know that…he didn't want to be humiliated.

JEAN: I'd rather he'd been humiliated, than…
(*Silence.*)

LES: You didn't help.

JEAN: What?

LES: The way you'd been carrying on.

JEAN: What do you mean?

LES: Ask Sylvia.

JEAN: About what?

LES: Sylvia and me, we had a talk last night.

JEAN: I'm surprised she could speak.

LES: She spoke enough to make me understand a bit more about Nick.

JEAN: What?

LES: She said that…that night…when they were out…he was in a pathetic state. Crying in his ale. (*Pause.*) He told her that he could have managed his job, and the drink would have been no problem, if it hadn't been for sex.

JEAN: What?

LES: He said sex was his only real problem, but it was fucking everything else up. If he wasn't getting hell from his wife, he was getting hell from you.

JEAN: That's not true.

LES: With you he'd looked for a second chance…but all he got was a second chain.

JEAN: That's not true!

LES: Isn't it?

JEAN: No.

LES: That's what Nick told Sylvia.

JEAN: If I chained him, it was because he wanted to be chained. (*Silence.*) He did want to be…

(*LES laughs. JEAN stares at him, then goes off in silence.*)

ANDY: I wonder where the bastard is.

LES: He mighta fucked off.

ANDY: Where?

LES: Anywhere.

ANDY: Anywhere?

LES: Africa.

ANDY: That's a long way.

LES: Further the better. Yeah…he might have shot through to Africa. He always said he'd like to take up white slave trading.

ANDY: I should've gone with him.

LES: What, slaving?

ANDY: No, trading. (*Pause.*)

LES: He could have jumped a steamer, you know.

ANDY: You think so? (*Pause.*) Pardon me while I trump. (*ANDY farts. Sits on the ramp, delicately.*) Had a rough night last night.

LES: Oh aye?

ANDY: Boozing and whoring. Paid for it this morning, though.

LES: How?

ANDY: The agony in the lavatory.

LES: (*Laughs.*) The squitters?

ANDY: What a way to start the day!

LES: What were you drinking?

ANDY: Home brewed stuff. Rotgut. (*Squirms.*) My arse feels like a blood orange. I feel as though I'm sitting on hot pips. Ohhh...I think I'll switch to pot in future. (*Pause.*) Where's Sylvie?

LES: Having her breakfast.

ANDY: All right?

LES: All right.

ANDY: You know Jean stayed here all night?

LES: Did she?

ANDY: She's in a bad state.

LES: Playing the tragedy queen.

(*ANDY looks through the binoculars.*)

ANDY: Yes, it's clearing up. (*Pause.*) I did something very strange this morning.

LES: What was that?

ANDY: Wiped my arse with my left hand.

LES: You musta been pissed.

ANDY: Very strange, that.

(*LES looks through the binoculars.*)

LES: When you think of all the people that get involved in anything like this...like the coastguards, and the helicopter pilot, and the ships...and the bloke who stayed up on the radio...and us...and oh, everyone...

ANDY: People want to help.

LES: I'd charge anyone who was rescued with the cost of the rescue.

ANDY: Oh, you spoilsport. (*Silence.*)

LES: Why couldn't she wait in the hotel?

ANDY: I suppose she wanted to be here.

LES: To greet Nick as he came dripping outa the fog?

ANDY: I suppose so.

LES: She's as crazy as he is. Huh... I think we're all crazy.

ANDY: How did you get on last night?

LES: All right.

ANDY: How is Sylvia?

LES: All right.

ANDY: You can't afford to take these things too seriously, can you?

LES: Which?

ANDY: I mean...it's okay, having a bit on the side... everyone has a bit on the side, every man does, naturally ...but you can't afford to let it upset you. I like a bit of strange as much as the next man, but I'd never let it interfere with the family. I think that was Nick's problem.

LES: What?

ANDY: I think you were right. Whatever Jean says, I think she wanted to get her hands on him for herself.

LES: Definitely.

ANDY: Nick said as much to me himself.

LES: Did he?

ANDY: She's been driving him up the wall of late. And you know where this...this expedition started?

LES: Where?

ANDY: Weeks ago...when we were planning the weekend. She suddenly announced she wanted to come on the weekend with us. Nick wouldn't hear of it.

LES: He didn't want her along?

ANDY: Never! But she kept bringing it up. She wasn't content to sit on the sidelines. She wanted to be with him all the time. I warned him it would happen. (*Pause.*) I'm sure she was even jealous of me! (*Pause.*) Then she said if he wouldn't take her he need not bother coming back.

LES: So he agreed...

ANDY: And then he came up with this idea.

LES: I see.

ANDY: I told him: Play around as much as you like, but don't let it spoil your family life. Don't let it affect the wife and kids...they're the ones that really count.

LES: How many kids have you got?

ANDY: Not enough.

LES: Eh?

ANDY: Never enough kids.

LES: How many?

ANDY: Four to date, but I'm working on the missus.

LES: You want more?

ANDY: Of course.

LES: And what about your missus?

ANDY: You know...people say a mother is closest to her children, but I don't accept that. I believe that a father is far closer. The times I have with those kids! You should come with us one Sunday.

LES: Where?

ANDY: The park. Every Sunday morning – about this time actually – I take them out to Mass, and then we go to the park and fool around. Makes no difference if it's raining or sunny, we enjoy ourselves. The oldest kicks a ball around – when I look at him I can see myself. I swear he'll make a centre-forward for Liverpool one day! And the little girl – she's only that high – she comes up to me and says: 'Daddy, I can't find any fairies in the grass!' And I help her to search for fairies in the grass! (*Laughing.*) Makes me feel young again. Yes, really... when I play with my kids, I say I'm doing it for their sake, but I'm not...I'm doing it for myself. I mean...it's keeping *me* young!

LES: Does your wife go with you?

ANDY: Their mother doesn't play with them like that. (*Pause.*) Marriage changes a woman more than it does a man. Mind you...they get on all right with her...

LES: How do you get on with her?

ANDY: Oh, she's a good woman. Good mother. I wouldn't hear a word said against her. (*Pause.*) But she's not the woman I love...

LES: Isn't she?

ANDY: No.

LES: Who's that?

ANDY: Oh, no one you would know. A woman I knew years ago in my teens. We had a marvellous relationship...

madly in love, both of us...but it just wasn't the right time for us. (*Pause.*) She got married and had a family...and I got married and had my family...

LES: Do you ever see her?

ANDY: I haven't seen her in ages. But after all these years and after hundreds of other women, I know that she was the one...of all of them, she was the one I really loved. I still do.

LES: Did you see Fat Annie?

ANDY: What?

LES: Last night...did you see Fat Annie?

ANDY: Oh, Annie...yeah...yeah, I saw her. I was standing in the pub, looking at the door, a plate glass door. And suddenly the glass went dark and a great shape blocked out the light.

LES: Fat Annie?

ANDY: Fatter Annie.

LES: Fatter?

ANDY: Yeah...fatter. Jesus, she was the one woman I would have sworn could never put on weight, she was that fat already.

LES: Does it turn you on?

ANDY: What?

LES: Her being that fat?

ANDY: No... (*Laughs.*) No, not really.

LES: But you fucked her?

ANDY: Yes.

LES: Did you fancy her?

ANDY: I didn't fancy her but I just couldn't resist the obscenity of it.

LES: Kinky.

ANDY: We lay in front of a roaring fire and I dined off roast arse.

LES: Tasty?

ANDY: My favourite dish...I'd eat it but for the hairs. (*They laugh.*)

LES: I should've come with you.

ANDY: Did you have a good night?

LES: Hilarious.

ANDY: (*Laughing.*) What did you do?

LES: Sylvia threw up in the bedroom so I cleaned it all up and put her to bed, and sat and drank a bottle of Scotch while she slept.

ANDY: I thought you were gonna have some wild sex.

LES: After last night?

ANDY: A reconciliation followed by a good fuck...nothing like it!

LES: Anyway she was unwell.

ANDY: What?

LES: She had the rags up.

ANDY: The best time of all!

LES: Eh?

ANDY: Women are always at their randiest during a period.

LES: Ugggh...

ANDY: What?

LES: All that blood!

ANDY: Shhh...

    (*SYLVIA comes on, walks down the ramp.*)

    Well...what have you got to say for yourself?

SYLVIA: What?

ANDY: (*Mock stern.*) Don't come the little innocent with me Miss. What about last night?

SYLVIA: What happened?

ANDY: Don't you know?

SYLVIA: My mind just blanked out.

ANDY: Just as well.

SYLVIA: What did I do?

ANDY: I'll spare you the memory.

    (*SYLVIA sits. ANDY looks through the binoculars.*)

    The ferry's coming in.

SYLVIA: When does it leave?

ANDY: About an hour or so.

SYLVIA: We'll have to catch it.

ANDY: You got to go back?

SYLVIA: Are you going to stay?

ANDY: I don't know. I think I'll go and talk to the coast-guards...

SYLVIA: If I wasn't back tonight my mother would have the police out after me. Anyway, I'll have to be back for work tomorrow.

ANDY: There's no call for that sort of language.

SYLVIA: What?

ANDY: 'Work'!

SYLVIA: I'm sorry. (*Pause.*) What are we going to do?

ANDY: What?

SYLVIA: About Nick?

ANDY: Order a wreath.

SYLVIA: Oh, Andy!

ANDY: I've been trying to decide between lilies and carnations.

SYLVIA: You're completely heartless.

ANDY: No disrespect.

SYLVIA: Huh…

ANDY: I mean, it comes to us all. You know, it's at times like this you really appreciate the value of your religion. It's funny…only last week I was in that little church near the Pier Head. Yes, I was passing, and I went in and knelt down for a bit. The alehouse was open and by rights I should have been in there. But I just had this impulse and I went in, and came out feeling strengthened.

SYLVIA: And then you went into the alehouse.

ANDY: Yes, and felt fortified.

SYLVIA: Nick wasn't religious, though, was he?

ANDY: Oh aye.

SYLVIA: He never talked about it.

ANDY: Oh, he had many failings but he still had his faith.

LES: We'll have to compose a message of condolence.

ANDY: We'll pick one out of the newspaper.

LES: 'Never forgotten, always rotten.' (*Silence.*)

ANDY: What if he turned up?

LES: Last we'll see of him.

SYLVIA: What?

LES: He's well away.

ANDY: Suppose he turned up and we'd all gone home?

LES: He could turn round and sail back.

SYLVIA: It would be awful, though, if he did turn up...

LES: Does it bother you?

SYLVIA: No, but...

LES: You wanna stay here?

SYLVIA: No. No.

(*Silence. ANDY stands.*)

ANDY: If we're gonna catch the ferry I'd better go and talk to Jean.

LES: She'll probably want to stay here.

ANDY: But we've all got responsibilities... I mean, we've got to get back, haven't we?

LES: She's got responsibilities too.

ANDY: We can't wait here indefinitely.

SYLVIA: She looks exhausted.

ANDY: She was stupid staying up all night.

(*Silence.*)

SYLVIA: I can't help feeling sorry for her.

LES: She'll take it out on her husband.

ANDY: You know...a thing like this makes you think. It reminds you of basic values. Take Nick. I mean, there he was...with a good wife, lovely kids, a good job. And he threw it all away. Why? He was always carrying on about being free. 'Free'...what the hell is that? He forgot the basic values...lost touch with his roots. Went haywire. I mean, you can take a drink without being an alcoholic. And you can have sex without being a sex maniac. But Nick...Nick really swallowed all this rubbish about permissiveness. Huh! Permission to what? Permission to ruin your life? Because that's what he did. (*Pause.*) Anyway, people are fed up with it now. It's not human, it's not real, it's just a fad. The pendulum is swinging back. It's already happened in America!

(*Silence. LES and SYLVIA look up at ANDY. ANDY stands still for a moment, then goes up the ramp and off. SYLVIA looks out to sea.*)

LES: (*Wry.*) 'The pendulum is swinging back.' (*Pause.*) You shoulda heard his sermon on the joys of fatherhood.

SYLVIA: He's always going on about his children.

LES: I wonder if there'll be any more fathers like him…in the future.

SYLVIA: He's very fond of his kids.

LES: He's a dying breed…poor bastard.

SYLVIA: What?

LES: When they grow up he'll be shattered.

SYLVIA: And what about you?

LES: What?

SYLVIA: When yours grow up…?

LES: I was shattered when they were born.

SYLVIA: Didn't you want a family?

LES: I never thought about it.

SYLVIA: But you did want them…at the time?

LES: I did and I didn't. (*Pause.*) I never thought much about it at the time.

SYLVIA: Did you discuss it with your wife?

LES: We just had them. (*Pause.*) Oh, I know it sounds crazy but…but everyone else had kids, it seemed to be the natural thing to do. It was only after they arrived I realised I didn't want them.

SYLVIA: How do you get on with them?

LES: All right.

SYLVIA: Do you?

LES: Yeah, I get on all right with them. I'm a model bad father, but I get on with them all right.
(*Pause.*)

SYLVIA: Don't you like children?

LES: It's not that.

SYLVIA: What then?

LES: I don't want to look after them.

SYLVIA: That's the woman's job.

LES: I don't want her to look after them then.

SYLVIA: It's natural for a woman to want children.

LES: What about Jean?

SYLVIA: What?

LES: She doesn't want children.

SYLVIA: She only says that because of Nick.

LES: Seems like everyone who wants them hasn't got them and everyone who's got them doesn't want them.
(*Silence.*)

SYLVIA: Les…

LES: What?

SYLVIA: About last night…

LES: Oh, skip it.

SYLVIA: I'm sorry.

LES: Doesn't matter.

SYLVIA: I want it to matter. (*Pause.*) I think I'm beginning to understand you a bit better now.

LES: What is there to understand?

SYLVIA: You won't flare up?

LES: Do you wanna go back to the hotel?

SYLVIA: I want to talk. (*Silence.*) What happened with Nick didn't matter. It didn't matter to me.

LES: Didn't it?

SYLVIA: No.

LES: That's all right, then.

SYLVIA: You're still mad.

LES: I'm not mad.

SYLVIA: You are…aren't you? (*Silence.*)

LES: The best relationship I ever had with a woman was with a prostitute I met in Hamburg. I couldn't speak a word of German, and she couldn't speak any English. I stayed with her every night for a fortnight. Sixty marks a night was the going rate. And in the morning she used to give me hot brutwurst with bags of mustard.

SYLVIA: Brutwurst?

LES: Sausages.

SYLVIA: Oh…

LES: The last morning she cried.

SYLVIA: She cried?

LES: Yes…I think I cried a bit too. But five minutes later my tears dried up, and I knew hers had too. (*Pause.*) That was the best relationship I ever had with a woman.
(*Silence.*)

SYLVIA: Don't be bitter.

LES: You think that's bitter? (*Laughs.*) It's a treasured memory, sweetheart. (*Pause.*) Nick's out of it all, now. In a way I almost admire him. (*Silence.*) Why do you think Nick took the dinghy?

SYLVIA: He liked sailing.

LES: Huh!

SYLVIA: He did!

LES: You know Andy wanted to sail with him?

SYLVIA: No.

LES: He did.

SYLVIA: I'd never have expected Andy –

LES: He was dead keen, but Nick insisted on sailing solo.

SYLVIA: Nick lives in a dream world.

LES: So does Andy.

SYLVIA: He doesn't strike me like that.

LES: All that crap he comes out with!

SYLVIA: What?

LES: He's dead.

SYLVIA: Dead?

LES: He goes to church and his faith is dead. He has women, and the sex is dead. He worships his family, and that's dead. You know he and his wife are always at each other's throats? I saw her one Saturday morning at the supermarket and she had a black eye and a mouthful of blood.

SYLVIA: I'd never have thought of Andy as violent.

LES: The only difference between Andy and Nick was that Nick didn't fool himself. He fooled almost everyone else but I don't think he fooled himself. (*Silence.*)

SYLVIA: I think all of you got married too young.

LES: You mean we should have waited?

SYLVIA: Yes.

LES: At least it would have shortened the agony. (*LES laughs.*)

SYLVIA: Do you think we would end up like that?

LES: Like what?

SYLVIA: Like Andy…or Nick…

LES: Or me?

SYLVIA: You're different. (*Pause.*) You are different.

LES: I'm no different. (*Silence.*)

SYLVIA: Have you ever had a fight with your wife?

LES: Yeah.

SYLVIA: A physical fight?

LES: Yes. That's what puts me off...

SYLVIA: What?

LES: You and me.

SYLVIA: We wouldn't...we wouldn't have to get married.

LES: It's not marriage.

SYLVIA: What is it then?

LES: I don't know. (*Pause.*) Can you understand me when I say that, if my mates had told me some fantastically sexy bird had fallen madly in love with me and was dying to meet me...then I would have run a mile?

SYLVIA: Oh aye...

LES: I would.

SYLVIA: Why?

LES: That's not what I want.

SYLVIA: What do you want?

LES: I don't want that. (*Silence.*)

SYLVIA: Did you ever fancy going with Nick?

LES: Sailing?

SYLVIA: Yes.

LES: No chance!

SYLVIA: But you knew more about sailing than any of them.

LES: I gave up sailing when I left the Navy.

SYLVIA: Do you ever think of going back in?

LES: I've had all that. (*Pause.*)

SYLVIA: I am sorry about...about Nick, and...

LES: It was bound to happen.

SYLVIA: It wasn't!

LES: If it hadn't been you it would have been me.
   (*Pause.*)

SYLVIA: Les...

LES: What?

SYLVIA: I would like to go on seeing you.

LES: So would I.

SYLVIA: But...is there any point?

LES: What?

SYLVIA: What is there to look forward to?

LES: Now?

SYLVIA: Yes.

LES: Nothing.

SYLVIA: Nothing?

LES: Nothing except seeing each other.

SYLVIA: I don't think that's enough.

LES: What do you want? A guarantee?

SYLVIA: No.

LES: I mean, how can I say...how do I know... Oh, Christ.
   (*Silence.*)

SYLVIA: There isn't anyone else, is there?

LES: Only my wife.

SYLVIA: I don't mean that.

LES: No.

SYLVIA: D'you think we ought to finish?

LES: All right.

SYLVIA: You want us to finish?

LES: As long as I can see you tomorrow.

SYLVIA: What?

LES: I don't mind parting forever as long as I can see you
   tomorrow.

SYLVIA: Oh, Les.
   (*SYLVIA sobs, kisses LES. JEAN comes on.*)

JEAN: It's all right!

SYLVIA: What?

JEAN: They're coming in now!

LES: What?
   (*JEAN seizes the binoculars. Peers out to sea, then runs up
   the ramp and looks from the promenade.*)

SYLVIA: Oh thank God...

LES: Who told you?

JEAN: A porter at the hotel. The coastguards have sent a
   motor launch out.
   (*LES joins JEAN.*)

LES: Can I have a look?
   (*JEAN gives him the binoculars and he looks.*)

There's something there...

JEAN: Let me see.

(*LES returns the binoculars.*)

LES: It's only a speck...

JEAN: Where? I can't see...

(*LES points. JEAN stands on the railing.*)

LES: Over there...could be anything.

JEAN: I see it. I see it!

LES: What is it?

JEAN: It's a small boat.

LES: Can I have a look?

(*LES peers through the binoculars. SYLVIA rushes up the rump and hugs JEAN.*)

SYLVIA: When did you hear?

JEAN: Now. Only just now.

LES: It's the launch. Towing the dinghy in.

JEAN: Oh, let me see! (*JEAN looks.*)

LES: See it?

JEAN: I see the launch...and oh God, yes, there's the dinghy.

(*ANDY comes along the promenade to the ramp. JEAN sees him, hugs him. She looks out to sea again through the binoculars.*)

SYLVIA: Can I see? (*SYLVIA looks through the binoculars.*) Oh, there they are!

(*SYLVIA hugs JEAN, both sobbing and laughing.*)

JEAN: Oh thank God...I'd never have forgiven myself if...if... All last night I sat there and all I could think was, 'He's gone.' All I could say to myself over and over again was, 'He's gone...he's gone.' And I...and I thought of the last time we were together...a row. We had a stupid row...I was crazy with jealousy, I couldn't stop myself...I saw how selfish I'd been...when he was crying out for help all I could see were my own miseries. (*Sobs.*) With all the problems he had, I wasn't helping him. I knew he needed me but instead of helping him I was destroying him...

(*As she speaks ANDY joins LES.*)

ANDY: She doesn't know.

LES: What?

ANDY: The boat was empty.

LES: Empty?

ANDY: Riding on the sea anchor.

LES: Oh Christ…

ANDY: All they're bringing in is the boat.

(*LES looks up at JEAN in silence.*)

LES: You better tell her.

(*JEAN stands high on the ramp.*)

JEAN: I was so selfish I couldn't see how desperate he was himself. I couldn't help him. But now I know…yes, now I know…

Blackout.

THE PUNISHMENT

Characters

THE HEADMASTER

ANTHONY

The Punishment was first produced by BBC 2 TV in 1972.

An office lined with books of classical literature. There is a desk with an armchair behind it and a plain chair in front. On the desk is a steel ruler and a copy of 'The Tablet'.

The HEADMASTER, a Jesuit priest in his sixties, sits at the desk looking through a set of school reports. There is a knock at the door. The HEADMASTER takes off his spectacles and looks at the door. After a pause the knock is repeated. The HEADMASTER stands.

HEADMASTER: Come.
> *(Pause. The HEADMASTER goes to the door. The door opens and ANTHONY comes in. He is about seventeen, strongly built and bigger than the HEADMASTER. He looks nervously at the HEADMASTER.)*
> Close the door, boy.
> *(ANTHONY closes the door. The HEADMASTER looks at him, then takes him by the arm in a strong grip and leads him to the desk. Stands there for a moment, still holding him by the arm.)*
> I hope this hasn't proved frightfully awkward for you…?

ANTHONY: What, father?

HEADMASTER: Coming in during the holidays…

ANTHONY: No, father.

HEADMASTER: It hasn't interfered with the family holidays?

ANTHONY: No, father.

HEADMASTER: Did you tell your family you were coming in?

ANTHONY: No, father.

HEADMASTER: I see. *(The HEADMASTER releases ANTHONY.)* Sit down.
> *(ANTHONY sits. The HEADMASTER stands looking at him.)*
> You look very pale. Not ill, are you?

ANTHONY: No, father.

HEADMASTER: I wouldn't want to think I'd brought you in if you were ill.

ANTHONY: No, father.

HEADMASTER: I thought it best to deal with a matter of this seriousness during the holidays. Have you told your parents?

203

ANTHONY: No, father

HEADMASTER: No? I See.

> (*Silence. The HEADMASTER toys with his spectacles. Looks at ANTHONY.*)
>
> Why? Why not?
>
> (*Silence.*)
>
> Were you ashamed?
>
> (*Silence.*)
>
> You weren't ashamed?

ANTHONY: Yes, father.

HEADMASTER: Hmmmm…yes.

> (*Silence.*)
>
> Were you frightened? Were you frightened, perhaps, of what, your father might do? I should imagine you'd have cause to be at least a little apprehensive, hmmm?

ANTHONY: Yes, father.

HEADMASTER: And what would your father have done?

> (*ANTHONY looks uncertain.*)
>
> What would you have expected him to do?
>
> (*Pause.*)
>
> Would he have beaten you?

ANTHONY: No, father.

HEADMASTER: No?

ANTHONY: No, father.

HEADMASTER: But he would have punished you?

ANTHONY: Yes, father.

HEADMASTER: If you had told him…what do you think he *ought to* have done? In what way would he best fulfil his moral obligation as a parent? Hmmm?

ANTHONY: I don't know, father.

HEADMASTER: And in what way would I best fulfil my moral obligation as a teacher? A moral obligation distinct from but complementary to that of the father…although perhaps in your case, in view of your failure to inform your parents, it might be best regarded as being exercised *in loco parentis*…what?

ANTHONY: Yes, father.

HEADMASTER: Although of course it might well be argued that while my moral obligation *qua* teacher demands that I punish you directly, it also demands that I inform your parents to enable them to carry out their moral obligation too...*qua parentes*? What?

ANTHONY: Yes, father.

(*Silence.*)

HEADMASTER: You see, Cunningham...you are not a genius.

ANTHONY: No, father.

HEADMASTER: (*Chuckling.*) You have no doubts about that?

ANTHONY: No, father.

HEADMASTER: A genius may be entitled to certain dispensations to enable him to fulfil his ordained role...and then again he may not. But you, Cunningham, are not a genius.

ANTHONY: No, father.

HEADMASTER: You are a perfectly ordinary boy with the usual quota of nasty appetites and mediocre abilities.

(*Silence.*)

Of course you are more inclined to indulge your appetites than to exercise your abilities. Which is true of course of the society in which we live...but that is all the more reason why you must learn to resist it now. *Now,* Cunningham, you understand...

It is my duty to help you to discipline those nasty appetites to which flesh is heir...and to exercise those abilities...however mediocre...which God has given you. I have spent many nights debating with myself...trying to free my mind of any prejudice or personal feelings of anger or disappointment in you...in order to clarify what my duty requires me to do.

I have prayed for guidance.

And I have prayed for you.

ANTHONY: Thank you, father.

(*Silence. The HEADMASTER toys with his spectacles.*)

HEADMASTER: You may be sure that my judgment is in no way affected by my personal feelings...

ANTHONY: No, father.

HEADMASTER: ...which is not to say that I have not experienced the deepest feelings of disappointment and shame at what you did. Shame...because I felt that in some way I must have failed you. I was ashamed of *my* failure. In a moment of weakness I even found myself wishing that I had never set foot inside the Prefects' Room that day...had never walked in and seen you...

ANTHONY: Yes, father.

HEADMASTER: Seen you, boy...

ANTHONY: Yes, father.

(*Silence.*)

HEADMASTER: And yet you denied it. When I asked you, you denied it...

ANTHONY: Yes, father.

HEADMASTER: You lied to me, Cunningham.

ANTHONY: Yes, father.

HEADMASTER: *Corruptio optimi pessima!* (*Pause.*) That night I prayed. I prayed for you.

ANTHONY: Thank you, father.

HEADMASTER: I prayed God to give you strength to admit the truth...hoping that you might erase the lie, if not the guilt. And by the grace of God you did so...but do you know what I should have had to do had you persisted in the lie?

ANTHONY: No, father.

HEADMASTER: I should have had no choice but to expel you on the spot.

ANTHONY: Yes, father.

HEADMASTER: And would that have seemed a reasonable and just punishment?

(*Silence.*)

Would that have seemed just, to you? Answer me, boy.

ANTHONY: Yes, father.

HEADMASTER: Yet knowing that...knowing the inevitable consequence...you still...

(*Silence.*)

Tell me, Cunningham. Would it surprise you to learn that you were to be expelled *now?*

ANTHONY: No, father.

HEADMASTER: Ahhh…then at least you do realize the
gravity of your offence. Quite apart from the lie…

ANTHONY: Yes, father.

HEADMASTER: A glimmer of hope there!

(*The HEADMASTER parades round the office, occasionally
stopping behind ANTHONY.*)

Of course we could forget it ever happened. No doubt you
would prefer that. Would you prefer that, Cunningham?

ANTHONY: No, father.

HEADMASTER: A positive gleam! It's something that you
realize that you must pay for your actions. There's hope
in that. If you consider that you must always pay, you
may find it less difficult to control your appetites in
future.

(*Pause.*)

Equally, I must bear in mind the influence *you* have on
the other boys. If you behave like that in the Prefects'
Room, what effect do you have on the others? Is it not
true that they will be inclined to do the same?

ANTHONY: Yes, father.

HEADMASTER: Which compounds the offence, and the
guilt. And if the Prefects behave like that, then what of
the boys themselves? Do you understand, Cunningham?

ANTHONY: Yes, father.

HEADMASTER: Ahhh…you do? Good. Then you may
begin to understand the meaning of responsibility. You
understand why it was essential that you be demoted
from your position as Prefect as soon as you admitted
the truth?

ANTHONY: Yes, father.

HEADMASTER: And, of course, I have borne that in mind
in considering how you should be punished. (*Pause.*) It
would be easier for me to send you out into the world,
where you could be employed making biscuits or
motorcars and perhaps even achieve some meretricious
success in commerce. It would be easier, and perhaps
even better for the school…but my duty is to produce

young men of moral backbone and religious conviction...with at least some pretension to intellectual rigour. You do understand, Cunningham?

ANTHONY: Yes, father.

HEADMASTER: And therefore it behoves me...

(*Pause. The HEADMASTER flicks through the School Reports.*)

Your attendance record is excellent.

ANTHONY: Thank you, father.

HEADMASTER: Your classroom behaviour generally considered good.

ANTHONY: Thank you, father.

(*Pause.*)

HEADMASTER: Do you have a 'girlfriend'?

ANTHONY: What, father?

HEADMASTER: A 'girlfriend'?

ANTHONY: Yes, father.

HEADMASTER: The Sports Master notes some lack of enthusiasm recently for attendance at evening or weekend events.

ANTHONY: Yes, father.

HEADMASTER: And just this term...you've been a little remiss about homework.

ANTHONY: Yes, father.

HEADMASTER: Do you see her frequently?

ANTHONY: Yes, father.

HEADMASTER: What? Every day?

ANTHONY: Yes, father.

HEADMASTER: Is she a Catholic?

ANTHONY: Yes, father.

(*Silence. The HEADMASTER concentrates on the reports.*)

HEADMASTER: I have decided that really the choice must be yours.

ANTHONY: What, father?

HEADMASTER: Undoubtedly you show a tentative talent for classical subjects.

ANTHONY: Thank you, father.

HEADMASTER: That is something worth encouragement... when most of the boys aspire to the sloppiness of modern literature or even worse, to messing about with test tubes, or doing sums.

ANTHONY: Yes, father.

HEADMASTER: You hope to take Classical Studies at Cambridge…

ANTHONY: Yes, father.

HEADMASTER: Have you been working during the holidays?

ANTHONY: Yes, father.

HEADMASTER: And have you been seeing this 'girlfriend'?

ANTHONY: Yes, father.

HEADMASTER: Frequently?

ANTHONY: Yes, father.

HEADMASTER: Is she on holiday too?

ANTHONY: Yes, father.

HEADMASTER: So that you do see quite a lot of each other?

ANTHONY: Yes, father.

HEADMASTER: Hmmm…of course, your prospects of getting a scholarship to Cambridge are extremely slim.

ANTHONY: Yes, father.

HEADMASTER: Even if, with God's grace, you did reasonably well in the examinations, you would still face enormous competition.

ANTHONY: Yes, father.

HEADMASTER: So much depends on the Headmaster's Report.

(*Silence. The HEADMASTER studies ANTHONY.*)

You do realize that, do you?

ANTHONY: Yes, father.

HEADMASTER: The question I have to ask myself in all conscience is: Can I honestly submit a favourable report of Cunningham? Will he make full use of the opportunities for academic study afforded by Cambridge? Or will he waste them? Will he be a good and improving influence upon his fellow students, or a bad one? What of his character? Do you understand my dilemma, boy?

ANTHONY: Yes, father.

HEADMASTER: I remember quite a few promising young men of my own generation who were ruined at Oxford.

ANTHONY: Yes, father.

HEADMASTER: I must be certain that your character is strong and trustworthy.

ANTHONY: Yes, father.

HEADMASTER: Of course you could always go to one of these redbrick universities, I suppose. No doubt they would take you in. (*Pause.*) Would you like to do that?

ANTHONY: No, father.

HEADMASTER: This 'girlfriend'...

(*Pause.*)

ANTHONY: Yes, father?

HEADMASTER: Is she hoping to go to university?

ANTHONY: Yes, father.

HEADMASTER: I see. You know, it's very silly of you to neglect your homework...or for that matter to be slack about games. You do understand that?

ANTHONY: Yes, father.

HEADMASTER: And now this... (*Pause.*) It's ground lost, boy...lost ground. I really do think that for the next year or so you would be wise to concentrate on your studies. Do you understand, Cunningham?

ANTHONY: Yes, father.

HEADMASTER: You agree?

ANTHONY: Yes, father.

HEADMASTER: Good.

(*Silence. The HEADMASTER takes hold of ANTHONY's arm, squeezes it tightly. ANTHONY winces.*)

(*Hearty.*) I suppose you think this is all an infernal fuss about a very minor transgression?

ANTHONY: No, father.

HEADMASTER: No?

ANTHONY: No, father.

HEADMASTER: Hmmm. (*Pause.*) You are not the first boy to report to this office during the holidays. You have many predecessors. Hum. (*Chuckling.*) No, by no means the first. Some of them now eminent names...men who have made their mark in classical scholarship, in research, and in one case in theology, Heaven help us. Tell me, Cunningham...do you have any idea what you would like to do eventually? Do you 'cherish any ambition', as they say?

ANTHONY: No, father.

HEADMASTER: Good. All too soon, Cunningham, the world closes in. All too soon you will find yourself wrestling with the cares of money and manhood and marriage...although of course marriage is a blessed sacrament...but at this stage you should be concerned to lay the foundation for your future.

ANTHONY: Yes, father.

HEADMASTER: Nothing can rival the study of Greek as a means of developing the capacity for logical analysis and cultivating the qualities of precision and clarity.

ANTHONY: No, father.

HEADMASTER: You are indeed fortunate to have the benefit of a classical education.

ANTHONY: Yes, father.

HEADMASTER: Of course the college has produced its quota of bakers, butchers, doctors and journalists...all manner of tradesmen...but I think we may be proud of our record in the disciplines that matter.

ANTHONY: Yes, father.

HEADMASTER: I doubt, Cunningham, that you are a natural leader...*capax imperii.*

ANTHONY: No, father.

HEADMASTER: But you may yet make a scholar. Yes, God willing, you may make a scholar yet. If, that is, you have the character...if you can close your ears to the whispers of temptation and dedicate yourself to the pursuit of truth. If you can accept this lapse as a warning...a warning of weakness...do you understand, Cunningham? (*The HEADMASTER seizes ANTHONY urgently by the arm and leans close to look at him.*)

ANTHONY: Yes...yes, father.

HEADMASTER: (*Intense.*) Nothing is achieved without suffering...without sacrifice.

(*Silence.*)

Are you truly sorry, Cunningham?

ANTHONY: Yes, father.

HEADMASTER: Then pray with me for forgiveness.

(*The HEADMASTER puts his hand on ANTHONY's shoulder, pressing him down.*

ANTHONY kneels.

The HEADMASTER put his hand on ANTHONY's head and begins a prayer of contrition.

ANTHONY whispers the prayer too.)

O my God...I am sorry...and beg pardon for all my sins...and detest them above all things, because they offend Thine infinite goodness...

(*The HEADMASTER's voice fades to an unintelligible mumble. ANTHONY peers up at him. Silence. The HEADMASTER takes away his hand. Crosses the room deeply absorbed. Stands by the desk.*)

(*Looking away.*) In view of the flagrant irresponsibility of your offence committed in the Prefects' Common Room – and the betrayal of trust involved – it would be altogether just if you were to forfeit not only your position as Prefect, but also your place in the school itself, with of course the opportunity to compete in the examinations for entry into Cambridge. However, in view of your contrition and your sincere desire to make amends, I have decided to temper justice with mercy... I have decided to offer you a choice.

(*Silence. ANTHONY waits nervously. His hands are sweating. The HEADMASTER turns to him.*)

Stand up boy.

(*ANTHONY stands.*)

You may sit for the entry examination to a redbrick university and I am reasonably certain that your abilities will win you a place there.

Alternatively, you may wish to proceed with the original plan of sitting for the entry examination to Cambridge, supported of course by a letter of reference from myself. In that case you must accept some physical chastisement, partly as a punishment, and partly as an assurance that your character is what it appears to be.

(*Silence.*)

Do you understand, Cunningham?

ANTHONY: Yes, father.

HEADMASTER: The choice is yours. (*Pause.*) I think I may claim to have done all that I can for you...I have tried to explain the gravity of the situation and to clarify the issues involved, to enable you to reach whatever decision you think fit.

ANTHONY: Thank you, father.

(*Silence.*)

HEADMASTER: Have you any questions you wish to ask?

ANTHONY: I...no, father.

HEADMASTER: Then the choice is simple. (*Pause.*) Either you choose to go to a redbrick establishment...do you want to do that?

ANTHONY: No, father.

HEADMASTER: Or you choose to accept a beating and try for Cambridge...now do you want to do that?

ANTHONY: Yes, father.

(*The HEADMASTER looks at ANTHONY for a moment.*)

HEADMASTER: That is your decision?

ANTHONY: Yes, father.

HEADMASTER: Very well.

(*The HEADMASTER gets up from his armchair and stands behind it. He gestures for ANTHONY to come round to the chair. ANTHONY looks confused.*

The HEADMASTER gestures again and ANTHONY comes round and stands at the side of the chair. Pause.)

ANTHONY: Father?

HEADMASTER: Drop your trousers.

(*ANTHONY unfastens his belt and lowers his trousers. The HEADMASTER takes his arm and bends him across the arm of the chair.*)

Nine strokes.

(*The HEADMASTER picks up the ruler and wraps it in some pages of 'The Tablet.' He strikes ANTHONY nine times, with hard measured strokes. ANTHONY's eyes are closed and his hands grip the sides of the chair. The HEADMASTER counts as he strikes.*)

One...two...three...four...five...six...seven...eight...nine. (*The HEADMASTER stands back.*)

Get up.

(*ANTHONY gets up, slowly, in great pain.*)

Get dressed.

(*ANTHONY dresses. Throughout this, the HEADMASTER has his back turned and doesn't look at him.*)

Get out.

(*ANTHONY turns toward the door.*)

ANTHONY: Thank you, father.

HEADMASTER: Cunningham...

ANTHONY: (*Stops.*) Yes, father?

HEADMASTER: I want you to pray.

ANTHONY: Yes, father.

HEADMASTER: Pray regularly. Every day.

ANTHONY: Yes, father.

HEADMASTER: And concentrate on your Greek.

ANTHONY: Yes, father.

(*Pause. ANTHONY moves to the door. The HEADMASTER still has his back turned.*)

HEADMASTER: And Cunningham...

ANTHONY: Yes, father?

HEADMASTER: I have decided not to mention the incident to your parents.

ANTHONY: Thank you, father.

HEADMASTER: It's best forgotten. Do you understand?

ANTHONY: Yes, father.

HEADMASTER: I think you might be wise not to mention the incident to anyone.

ANTHONY: Yes, father... No.

HEADMASTER: Don't ever mention it. You understand? Never.

ANTHONY: No, father.

(*Silence. ANTHONY opens the door.*)

Thank you father.

(*ANTHONY goes and closes the door.*
The HEADMASTER turns, sits at the desk.
He slides the ruler out from inside the copy of 'The Tablet'
and places it on the desk. Then he unfolds the paper and
smoothes it.
He puts the pages back with the others.
He sits for a moment looking at the door.
Then he takes up 'The Tablet' and begins to read.)

End of Play.